D1099840

Collins

Your Life

Student Book 2

New fully revised 3rd edition

The whole-school solution for Citizenship and PSHE

Now fully covering
Economic wellbeing and
financial capability

John Foster and
Simon Foster

William Collins' dream of knowledge for all began with the publication of his first book in 1819. A self-educated mill worker, he not only enriched millions of lives, but also founded a flourishing publishing house. Today, staying true to his spirit, Collins books are packed with inspiration, innovation and practical expertise. They place you at the centre of a world of possibility and give you exactly what you need to explore it.

Collins. Do more.

Published by Collins
An imprint of HarperCollinsPublishers
77–85 Fulham Palace Road
Hammersmith
London
W6 8JB

Browse the complete Collins catalogue at
www.collinseducation.com

© HarperCollinsPublishers Limited 2005

10 9 8 7 6 5 4 3 2 1

ISBN 978-0-00-731246-7

John Foster asserts his moral right to be identified as the author of this work.

British Library Cataloguing in Publication Data
A Catalogue record for this book is available from the British Library.

Commissioned by: Charlie Evans

Edited by Kim Richardson

Design by Jordan Publishing Design
Layout by eMC Design Ltd

Cover design by Angela English

Printed and bound by Printing Express, Hong Kong

Production by Simon Moore

Mixed Sources
Product group from well-managed
forests and other controlled sources
www.fsc.org Cert no. SW-COC-1806
© 1996 Forest Stewardship Council

FSC is a non-profit international organisation established to promote the responsible management of the world's forests. Products carrying the FSC label are independently certified to assure consumers that they come from forests that are managed to meet the social, economic and ecological needs of present and future generations.

Find out more about HarperCollins and the environment at
www.harpercollins.co.uk/green

Contents

Your Life 1 is the first of three books which together form a comprehensive course in Personal, Social, Health and Economic Education (PSHEE) and Citizenship at Key Stage 3. The table shows how the fourteen PSHEE units cover the requirements for Personal wellbeing and Economic wellbeing and financial capability for 11–14 year olds and how the nine Citizenship units cover the National Curriculum for Citizenship at Key Stage 3.

Personal, Social, Health and Economic Education

Personal wellbeing – Understanding yourself and handling relationships	Personal wellbeing – Keeping healthy	Economic wellbeing and financial capability
These units concentrate on developing your self-knowledge and your ability to manage your emotions and how to handle your relationships.	These units are designed to complement the work on healthy living that you are doing elsewhere in the curriculum.	These units aim to help you to manage your money effectively, to learn about the world of work and to practise the skills involved in being enterprising.

- **You and your feelings** – self-esteem (Personal wellbeing 1.1a b 2.1b e)
- **You and your time** – making the most of your leisure (Personal wellbeing 2.1b 3f)
- **You and your family** – divided families (Personal wellbeing 1.4a c 2.3a b c 3i j)
- **You and other people** – friends and friendships (Personal wellbeing 1.4a c 2.3a b c)
- **You and other people** – older people (Personal wellbeing 1.5a b 2.3d 3m)
- **You and your achievements** – reviewing your progress (Personal wellbeing 2.1b d 3b 4f Economic wellbeing and financial capability 2.1d 3d)

- **You and your body** – drinking and alcohol (Personal wellbeing 2.2a b c e 3e)
- **You and your body** – contraception and safer sex (Personal wellbeing 2.2a 2.3b 3d)
- **You and your safety** – at home and in the street (Personal wellbeing 2.2a c d 3g h)
- **You and your body** – drugs and drugtaking (Personal wellbeing 1.2a 1.3a b 3e 4c)

- **You and your money** – gambling (Economic wellbeing and financial capability 1.2b 2.4a 4a)
- **You and the world of work** – employment and unemployment (Economic wellbeing and financial capability 1.1c 1.4a 2.2c 2.3a 3c e f)
- **You and the world of work** – understanding business (Economic wellbeing and financial capability 1.4a b 3j)

The various activities within each unit provide opportunities for you to learn how to grow as individuals, for example, by developing self-awareness and taking responsibility for managing your time. The group discussion activities involve you in learning how to work as a team and how to develop the skills of co-operation and negotiation. You are presented with situations in which you have to work with others, to analyse information, to consider moral and social dilemmas and to make choices and decisions.

Citizenship

Developing as a citizen

These units aim to develop your knowledge and understanding of the world around you, and to develop the skills that you will require as an active citizen.

- **You and your responsibilities** – other cultures and lifestyles
  (Citizenship 1.1c 1.3a b 2.1a b 3d i j)

- **You and your values** – where do you stand?
  (Citizenship 2.1a c 2.2a b c 4a)

- **You and the law** – the police
  (Citizenship 1.1b 2.1a c 3a b)

- **You and the community** – the school as a community
  (Citizenship 2.1a 2.2a b c d 4a b c d Economic wellbeing and financial capability 1.2b 1.3b)

- **You as a citizen** – of the European Union
  (Citizenship 1.3c 3k)

- **You and the media** – the power of advertising
  (Citizenship 3d i)

- **You and your opinions** – speaking your mind
  (Citizenship 2.1a b c 2.2a b c d 4a b)

- **You and global issues** – food and water
  (Citizenship 2.1a b 2.2a b c 4a g h)

- **You and the community** – taking action on the local environment
  (Citizenship 2.3a b c d 3e 4a b c d e)

Self-esteem and confidence

Self-esteem

What is self-esteem?

Self-esteem means having a good opinion of yourself. It is based on understanding what your strengths are and valuing yourself as a person.

Why is self-esteem important?

Self-esteem is important because it enables you to have the confidence to be yourself. If you have self-esteem, you will say what you think and do what you think is right, rather than say or do things in order to try to impress other people.

Having self-esteem will make you feel happier. You won't let people make you feel badly about yourself if they criticise you unfairly. Because you believe in yourself, you'll respect yourself and other people will respect you too. You won't fall into the trap of blaming yourself for everything that goes wrong in your life.

Self-esteem will give you the confidence to try new experiences. It will also help you to achieve more, because you will have a positive attitude that makes it easier to deal with setbacks.

Is self-esteem the same as conceit?

No. A conceited person has an exaggerated opinion of themselves. A person with self-esteem has a balanced view of their own worth, valuing their good points, but understanding that like everyone else they are not perfect.

Feeling Confident

Some people seem to be born confident. They can enter a crowded room, immediately feel at home and settle down and talk to anybody. Confidence comes from believing in yourself and feeling happy. Once you're confident about what you want out of life, you can go for it.

When you're confident about yourself – how you look and how you feel – many other problems disappear. Perhaps you have to read some of your work out in front of the whole class. If you feel confident in yourself, you'll be less pre-occupied with things that don't matter – like how you look and where you're sitting – and more concerned with making the reading interesting for the rest of the class.

Know *Yourself*

Make a list of what your strong points are. You can feel proud of what you're good at.

Not so good points	Good points
tidying room	making friends
getting to sports practice on time	swimming
handwriting	telling jokes
cleaning shoes	eating healthy food
nail biting	studying hard
brushing hair	organising games
washing dishes	painting
	staying fit

Feeling confident will show in the way you look

In pairs

On your own, make one list of the things you are good at, and another list of the things you think you're not so good at. Then show your lists to a partner. Go through the list of good points and discuss the things you've included that make you feel good and that you are most proud of. Then choose one of the things from your not so good list and discuss together something positive that you could do in order to get better at it.

self-esteem

In groups

Discuss the advice that Erica Stewart gives in her article. Which piece of advice is the most useful? Which is the hardest to put into practice?

What do you think?

Study the six statements below. Talk about each one in turn, saying why you agree or disagree with it. Make notes of your views and share them in a class discussion.

1 What other people think of you and your behaviour is more important than what you think yourself.

2 It's not being conceited to feel proud of yourself and your achievements.

3 It's not what you look like that matters, it's what kind of person you are and how you feel about yourself.

4 If you're not confident about doing something, it's better to avoid doing it rather than risk making a fool of yourself.

5 People who keep putting you down only do so to try to make themselves feel better.

6 Imitating people by doing whatever is regarded as cool and trendy is the best way to boost your confidence.

Erica Stewart offers tips on how to build up your self-esteem

1 Think positively

Look at things in a positive rather than a negative way. For example, if you do badly in a test, don't think: 'I'm hopeless. I'm never going to get a good mark.' Instead, think about what you can do to make sure you get a good mark next time, such as asking for extra help with things you don't understand.

2 Stand up for yourself

Make up your own mind about what you believe and stick to it. It's harder to say no than to say yes, but don't let your friends pressurise you into doing things you don't believe are right. Don't feel guilty or that you're letting them down. You'll respect yourself far more for sticking up for your beliefs than if you give in and do something just to please others. And other people will respect you far more, too.

3 Be realistic

Be realistic about what you can achieve. Don't set yourself unachievable targets. If you're really determined to do something, then go for it. But adopt a step-by-step approach, setting yourself a series of short-term goals and dates by which you plan to achieve each one.

4 Cope with criticism

If you're criticised, it can damage your self-esteem. Consider carefully whether the criticism is fair. For example, if you let the rest of the cast down by not turning up for an important play rehearsal, then accept that it was your fault. Apologise and reassure everyone that you won't let it happen again. But if you are being unfairly criticised, recognise what is going on and either ignore it or take steps to ensure that it doesn't continue.

5 Take risks

If you're not prepared to take risks then you cut down on the chances of having new experiences and finding out what you're capable of doing and achieving. Of course, that doesn't mean doing things that are dangerous or reckless. But avoiding taking any risks because you're afraid of making a fool of yourself won't do anything for your self-confidence. It's usually best to have a go. If it doesn't work out, you can always tell yourself that at least you tried.

7

Shyness

Coping with Shyness

Few people are strangers to shyness.

It sweeps over us in many situations: arriving at a party, talking in front of the class, starting a conversation with someone important or taking on a new task. Even something as 'simple' as ordering gig tickets over the phone for the first time or signing your name at the bank can make you feel awkward.

Shyness, one of the most complex and untalked about emotions, has many different effects. Dryness of the mouth, fumbling, stuttering, avoiding eye contact, not speaking up, blushing, feeling sick, sweating, headaches: it's no wonder the word most often coupled with shyness is 'crippling'. It can stop you accepting invitations, trying new experiences and getting on in life.

As a teenager you are at the peak of your self-consciousness, and shyness is a result of worrying about your image. You are looking and feeling different, experiencing new emotions and being put in more 'adult' situations. You want to deal with situations smoothly even though you've never encountered them before.

As you become older and more experienced a lot of the awkwardness you feel goes away. But you can help yourself now by recognising that the way you feel reflects your own thoughts. If you're down on yourself – 'No one likes me'; 'I look awful'; 'I never know what to say' – you are bound to feel shy.

How to beat shyness

- Shy body language can make situations worse. **Try to speak clearly** (mumble and you will be asked to repeat yourself) and look people in the eye.

- **Think positive.** Tell yourself you can cope and you will. Try and focus on what you like about yourself and what you are good at. For example, if you are a good skater, imagine yourself skating confidently.

- **Taking a deep breath** and relaxing will stop your mind working overtime. If your body is calm, you are less likely to fluff your words.

- Shy people are often seen as 'aloof' or 'off' because they stand alone and look unapproachable in social situations. Try to **break the ice** before your anxiety builds up, and don't put on a front.

- **Be realistic.** Just because you are feeling self-conscious doesn't mean everyone is looking at you or analysing your every word. Look at the situation rationally and realise that you are not the centre of attention.

- **Face the fear.** If you are scared of doing something, do it anyway. It's the only way to learn.

In groups

Discuss what you learn about shyness from the article on this page. Talk about what causes shyness and how it makes you feel.

Discuss the advice that is given on how to cope with shyness. Which do you think are the most useful of the tips?

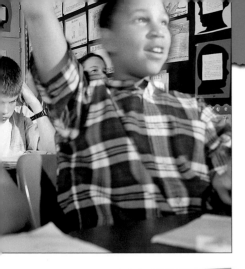

Making mistakes

Making a mistake can not only be embarrassing, but it can also damage your self-confidence. Everyone makes mistakes. So when you make a mistake, it's important to keep it in perspective and to learn from it.

Coping with classroom MISTAKES ✗

Embarrassment and fear of failure can hold you back from contributing in class. However, not speaking out has far-reaching effects outside the classroom. It can stop you standing up for yourself and your beliefs, and it can make you miss opportunities. If you let the fear of failure (the fear of getting something wrong or saying something embarrassing) overwhelm you at school, it will overwhelm you in everything you do.

The things to remember are:

✗ It's not the end of the world if you give an incorrect answer.

✗ Not understanding something isn't a sign of stupidity. Not asking for help is stupid.

✗ Embarrassment is only momentary.

✗ No one remembers the things you get wrong.

✗ Speaking in front of people gets easier the more you do it.

✗ If someone shouts you down, assert yourself and ask them to let you finish.

Learning from your mistakes

Growing up is all about experiencing things for the first time. It is easy to make a mistake because you are inexperienced.

If you make mistakes because you are careless, try and give more time to things. Take life more slowly. Think things out and plan how you're going to act.

If you think you might make mistakes because you feel uncertain or ignorant about something, talk about it with someone you trust. Don't act without a second opinion.

If you make mistakes because you're nervous, take a deep breath before you act. Don't panic yourself into acting on impulse or in a way which isn't really you, just because you think you must make your mark.

Concentrate on all the good things you can do, and don't dwell on things you aren't so good at. Making mistakes is all about lacking knowledge – and that's something you can work on putting right.

Don't blame yourself

If you blame yourself for everything that goes wrong, you'll soon begin to lose confidence in yourself.

But everybody makes mistakes. It's part of human nature. And if you can learn from where you went wrong, you'll become a wiser person.

✦ In groups

1 Talk about how to cope with classroom mistakes. Is it fair to make fun of people who make mistakes in class?

2 Discuss the advice on learning from your mistakes. What do you think is the most useful piece of advice?

For your file

Use the information in this unit as the basis for a short article for a teenage magazine explaining why it is important to have self-esteem and what you can do to build up your self-confidence.

9

Drugs – Facts and Fictions

66 Many young people who start taking drugs don't realise what they are getting into. There are lots of myths about drugtaking. Before you do anything rash, it's worth knowing all the facts and what risks are involved. 99
– *Drugs counsellor*

Only other people get hooked or hurt by drugs

Part of the problem with drugs is that most users think they're invincible. They believe that the dangers will never affect them because it's other people who end up being rushed to hospital, other people who can't handle the effects of drugs.

If you're someone who is tempted to take drugs, don't ignore the information and warnings. Drugs can and do kill. They don't discriminate – it could happen to anyone.

People get their drugs from pushers

Contrary to popular belief, most people come into contact with drugs through friends and older sisters or brothers, not through anonymous pushers on the street. What's more, being approached by someone you like makes saying no harder and more complicated.

All drugs are dangerous

The danger when taking drugs depends on many things, such as *what* you've taken, *how much* you've taken, and your state of mind at the time. Although some drugs are less dangerous than others, illegally manufactured drugs are *always* a danger because it's impossible to tell what's in them. Never trust a friend who tells you something is safe

because they've tried it. Everyone reacts differently to drugs – body size, weight, age and sex all need to be taken into account.

Soft drugs lead to hard drugs

One of the greatest myths of all time is that taking soft drugs automatically means you'll end up on hard drugs. There is no evidence to suggest that this is true, although taking any kind of drug does increase your chances of coming into contact with harder drugs. This is because drugs like Ecstasy, Speed and LSD are often mixed with other substances, and are often available through the same sources. What you have to remember with drugs is that you always have a choice. A choice not to take them, a choice to stop taking them and a choice not to go any further.

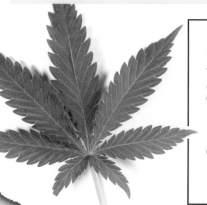

Is Cannabis Safe?

You may have heard people say cannabis is risk free. This isn't true.
- Heavy use of cannabis over a long period of time can lead to users relying on the drug as a way of relaxing and being sociable.
- **Heavy, long-term cannabis use can make you feel less energetic than normal. This can have a**

negative effect on the way you live your life.
- Smoking cannabis with tobacco causes lung damage. In fact it's reckoned that smoke from an unfiltered spliff carries more risks than a cigarette. However, people tend to smoke many more cigarettes than spliffs.

ECSTASY FACTFILE

Name: *The chemical name for ecstasy is MDMA.*

Form: *Ecstasy comes as tablets of different shapes, sizes and colours. Because it can look like many other drugs or medicines, a lot of people have been sold tablets which have turned out not to be ecstasy. Since you can never be quite sure what you are buying, a lot of people think buying ecstasy isn't worth the risk.*

Legal category: *Ecstasy is a Class A drug. It is illegal to possess or supply ecstasy.*

Effects: *Ecstasy is a stimulant which users say gives them a 'rush' feeling followed by a sense of calm, making them feel closer to other people and more aware of their surroundings. They get an energy buzz, which means they can dance for long periods. The effects begin about 20 minutes after they've taken a tablet and last for several hours.*

Risks: *As ecstasy starts to work people sometimes feel sick, their heart rate increases and their jaw muscles tighten. Some people become anxious and feel confused and frightened.*

Ecstasy raises the body's temperature. Dancing for a long time in a hot atmosphere after taking ecstasy can lead to overheating and dehydration (loss of too much body fluid). The risks can be reduced by 'chilling out' and taking regular breaks from dancing, and by drinking about a pint of a non-alcoholic fluid, such as water, fruit juice or a sports drink every hour. Users are advised to sip the drink regularly, to avoid alcohol and to eat salty food in order to replace the sodium they have lost through sweating.

Once the effects of the ecstasy wear off, users can feel tired and depressed, but may find it hard to sleep.

Research into the long-term effects of using ecstasy suggest that heavy use may cause damage to the brain, leading to depression and memory loss later in life. Use of ecstasy has also been linked to liver and kidney problems.

There have been around 50 deaths a year as a result of taking ecstasy. Evidence suggests that most were as a result of heatstroke.

For your file

Use the information on this page and write an article for a teenage magazine entitled 'Ecstasy – is it worth the risk?' Explain what physical effects ecstasy has – both pleasurable and harmful – and give your views on the risks involved in taking ecstasy.

In groups

What do you learn from these pages about the risks of drugtaking? Discuss the views of these young people (below) and say why you agree or disagree with them.

'Experimenting with drugs is too risky. You don't know what you're taking and how your body will react.'

'There's too much fuss about drugtaking. Most people who take drugs get a good feeling and it doesn't do them any harm.'

'Taking drugs is a waste of money. You don't need drugs in order to have a good time.'

In pairs

Study the article on ecstasy. Make a list of the important facts about ecstasy which you learn from the article.

Role play

Act out a situation in which a doctor explains to a teenager the risks involved in taking ecstasy and smoking cannabis.

Role play a scene in which two people argue about the risks of drugtaking – one saying it's worth the risk, the other saying it's not. Take it in turns to be the person saying it's not worth the risk.

Drugs and the Law

If the police have reason to suspect you're carrying an illegal drug they have the right to make you turn out your pockets. They can also take you to the police station and search you. If drugs are found, you could be charged with one of TWO offences.

1 Possession

This means being caught with an illegal drug for your own use. The police can tell your parents or carer. They could also inform the Social Services and the Probation Service. As for punishment, the police can give you either a reprimand, a warning or prosecute you (see page 39). If you are found guilty in court you can get a fine or a custodial sentence.

2 Possession with intent to supply drugs

If you had any intention of dealing (which can include giving and sharing drugs) you may be charged with this more serious offence. Decisions over whether you're charged with intent to supply are based on the circumstances in which you were caught and the quantity of drugs you were caught with. The police can take the same course of action as in simple possession cases, but this time you're more likely to be charged. If your case goes to court the penalties are likely to be heavier.

If you have a drugs record:

Obtaining a visa to travel to some countries may become difficult or could even be denied. It could affect your job prospects. When you're applying for a job, an employer may check if you have a criminal record or any past convictions. *Ignorance won't wash with the law.* The Misuse of Drugs Act divides drugs into three classes and gives guidance for penalties.

Class A

cocaine, crack, ecstasy, heroin, LSD (acid), magic mushrooms prepared for use, speed (amphetamines) if prepared for injection

Maximum Penalties:
● **possession:** 7 years' prison and/or unlimited fine
● **supply:** life imprisonment and/or unlimited fine

Class B

cannabis, speed (amphetamines)

Maximum Penalties:
● **possession:** 5 years' prison and/or unlimited fine
● **supply:** 14 years' prison and/or unlimited fine

Class C

rohypnol, supply of anabolic steroids and tranquillisers/possession of temazepam (mazzies)

Maximum Penalties:
● **possession:** 2 years' prison and/or unlimited fine
● **supply:** 14 years' prison and/or unlimited fine

In groups

Discuss what you learn from this page about the laws on drugs.

1 What can the police do if they think you are carrying drugs?

2 What offences could the police charge you with if you are caught carrying drugs?

3 Into what different classes does the law divide illegal drugs? How do the maximum sentences differ according to which class a drug is in?

4 What can be the consequences of having a drugs record?

5 How effective do you think the current drugs laws are? Do you think they act as a deterrent? What effect do you think they have on the way drugtakers obtain and use drugs?

6 Do you think the drugs laws should be changed in any way?

Should there be harsher penalties for supplying drugs? What are the arguments for and against making drug use legal and allowing people to possess drugs in small amounts for their own personal use?

For your file

Write a statement giving your views on the drugs laws.

Saying 'no' to drugs

🔘 In groups

Talk about all the different situations in which a teenager might be offered drugs. Why might they choose to refuse or accept? Talk about factors that might influence their decision, such as where they are, who they are with, what mood they are in and how much pressure is put on them to join in.

Discuss the advice which the extract gives on how to turn down drugs and stay friends. Which piece of advice do you think is the most helpful?

◁▷ Role play

Role play a scene in which a teenager is being offered drugs and a group of their friends is putting pressure on them to accept. Discuss various tactics that the teenager can use in order to say no. Is it best to just say no and walk away? To state clearly the reasons why you personally don't want to take them? To argue with the people who are offering them to you, and try to stop them taking any?

Take it in turns to be the person being pressurised, and discuss which of the tactics worked most successfully.

How to turn down drugs and stay friends

▶ Say no and don't feel bad about it. Obsessing about what you've said, how you've said it, and what people think of you is bad news.

▶ Being the only non drug-taker may feel awkward and uncomfortable but this is just a phase and, like all awkward phases, it will pass.

▶ Don't make things worse for yourself by letting your imagination exaggerate a situation. Being the odd one out is hard but it doesn't mean your friends no longer like you.

❝ *When I refused to smoke drugs at a party, I thought all my friends thought I was being stupid. I got so upset about it that I went home early and cried. Over the weekend I decided that if they didn't like me for not taking drugs, I wasn't going to be friends with them any more. When I got to school on Monday, I was all ready to fight with them but then I found out they were all worried about me and had no idea why I'd got so upset.* ❞

▶ Strange, but true, no one is judging you. Everyone is so worried about themselves and how they look to other people that they aren't even thinking about you.

▶ Question people who try to bully you into taking drugs. After all, if drugs are so brilliant, why is it so necessary for them to have your company? If someone is giving you grief for saying no, ask them the following:

➡ Why is it so important for you to take them?

➡ Why are they so stressed out about you saying no?

➡ Why do they have to make other people take them too?

Britain
a diverse society

Today, Britain is a diverse society consisting of people from many different ethnic backgrounds.

The origins of the ethnic diversity in modern Britain lie in the immigration that has taken place from various parts of the world. Many immigrants came to Britain in the years following the end of the Second World War in 1945. During the 1950s and 1960s large numbers of people came to Britain from the Caribbean and from South Asia. Immigration was encouraged during these years because workers were needed to help rebuild the British economy after the war.

In addition to West Indians, Indians, Pakistanis and Bangladeshis, there are important immigrant groups in Britain of Americans, Canadians, Australians, Italians, Greeks, Turkish Cypriots and Chinese.

In 2001, there were 4 million people from ethnic minorities living in Britain. This represented 7% of the total population.

In recent years the UK population has become increasingly diverse. In 2006, 90% of the UK population of 60 million were white, compared to 93% in 2001.

Asians were the largest ethnic minority group with 5% of the population.

The ethnic minority population is concentrated in the larger cities. In London one third of the population is from ethnic minority groups.

Almost 20% of schoolchildren in the UK were from ethnic minorities groups, and 50% in London.

People from ethnic minorities have introduced their own cultures and lifestyles to Britain. Members of their communities have made significant contributions to society in all walks of life – industry and commerce, medicine and science, politics, the media, arts and sports.

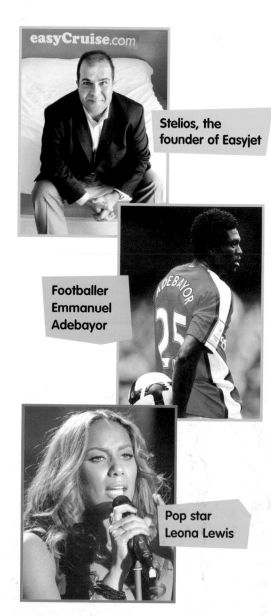

Stelios, the founder of Easyjet

Footballer Emmanuel Adebayor

Pop star Leona Lewis

In groups

Discuss what you learn from this page about ethnic diversity in Britain today.

Ethnic stereotyping

It is important not only to respect other people's cultures and lifestyles, but also not to discriminate against them by stereotyping them. **Ethnic stereotyping** means thinking that all people from the same ethnic background have similar characteristics and behave in exactly the same way.

> ❝ I was singing an Asian song with a friend, and my best friend – she's Afro-Caribbean – said, 'Don't tell me you're one of those?' I said to her, 'One of what?' She replied, 'You know, TP,' and I asked her, 'What's TP?' She said, 'Typical Paki.' I answered her, 'So what, I'm proud of what I am. ❞
> – Nazrah

> ❝ My friend Asif's a really good footballer. But lots of the other kids say he'll never get anywhere because there's this idea that Asian boys haven't got what it takes to become professional footballers. ❞ – Tariq

In groups

1 Discuss Nazrah's comment. Are young people from ethnic minorities sometimes stereotyped because of the music they like? Are people sometimes stereotyped because of the way they dress?

2 Discuss Tariq's comment. Then read and discuss John Agard's poem 'Stereotype'. Talk about the stereotypical views that people have of what people from different ethnic groups are good at doing.

3 Talk about national stereotypes, for example, the views that other people sometimes have of English people as either stiff, cold and unfriendly, or as aggressive, beer-drinking football hooligans. What stereotypes are there of **a)** Scottish, **b)** French, **c)** German people? Discuss how these stereotypes have come about and why they present a false image.

Stereotype

I'm a fullblooded
West Indian stereotype
See me straw hat?
Watch it good

I'm a fullblooded
West Indian stereotype
You ask
if I got riddum
in me blood
You going ask!
Man just beat de drum
and don't forget
to pour de rum

I'm a fullblooded
West Indian stereotype
You say

I suppose you can show
us the limbo, can't you?
How you know!
How you know!
You sure
you don't want me
sing you a calypso too
How about that

I'm a fullblooded
West Indian stereotype
You call me
happy-go-lucky
Yes that's me
dressing fancy
and chasing woman
if you think ah lie
bring yuh sister

I'm a fullblooded
West Indian stereotype
You wonder
where do you people
get such riddum
could it be the sunshine
My goodness
just listen to that
steelband

Isn't there one thing
you forgot to ask
go on man ask ask
This native will answer
anything
How about cricket?
I suppose you're good at
it?

Hear this man
good at it!
Put de willow
in me hand
and watch me stripe
de boundary

Yes I'm a fullblooded
West Indian stereotype

that's why I
graduated from Oxford
University
with a degree
in anthropology

John Agard

Images and stereotypes

Negative stereotyping

For many years the only way in which black people appeared in Hollywood films was as servants – house cleaners, cooks, gardeners – or in other humble forms of employment. They were never shown as important, powerful or clever people. Nor were they shown as having an individual personality.

The Chinese – in fact most people from Asia – were also only seen in certain stereotypical roles. They were portrayed as untrustworthy, cruel, pathetically over-polite, or associated with opium dens. In these ways certain ethnic groups come to be seen only in crude caricature, like cartoon characters. Their existence, as real people with real lives and real feelings and thoughts, became invisible.

Black people underrepresented on TV says Lenny Henry

In a speech to the Royal Television Society, Lenny Henry attacked the BBC and ITV for not employing enough black staff behind the screen as well as on it.

He also criticised underrepresentation of minorities in soaps, such as Coronation Street.

He called on TV bosses to use 'affirmative action' to employ more black people, adding: 'And I am not talking about cleaners, security guys, scene-shifters – I am talking about decision-makers.'

In groups

1 Discuss what is meant by **negative stereotyping** and how films used to present negative stereotypes of people from ethnic minorities.

2 Study the article from the *Coventry Telegraph*. Do you agree with the views expressed by the people who were interviewed, that TV programmes do not reflect the multi-cultural nature of society?

3 Talk about recent TV programmes and films which have featured people from ethnic minorities. Discuss how the characters were portrayed and whether or not you think they were stereotypes.

4 Choose a popular TV soap, and share ideas for introducing two new characters from an ethnic minority background. Discuss how you would integrate them into the story in order to present a true picture of what life is like for people from their background in Britain today.

Top Soaps Accused Of Stereotyping Ethnic Minorities

Coronation Street and EastEnders have been accused of stereotyping ethnic minorities.

Viewers cited Asian corner shop owner Dev in Coronation Street and single mother Denise, who had two children by different fathers in EastEnders, as examples of stereotyping and tokenism in soaps.

The report was commissioned by Channel 4 following the furore over the allegedly racial abuse of Bollywood star Shilpa Shetty on Celebrity Big Brother. Ethnic minority viewers accused all broadcasters of tokenism and stereotyping, screening exaggerated and extreme representations of minorities and failing to reflect modern ethnic minority culture.

A distorted picture?
Does the media stereotype Africans?

'Media images of Africans always seem to be starving children, war, uneducated people or scenes of poverty. But not all of Africa is poor, in fact many countries are very modern. African children are shown as living a tough life and having to grow up quickly. Obviously there are some children in that position, but it's not a depressing life for all of them.' – Sekai Makoni, 14

'Of course Africans are stereotyped. The media portrays Africans as poor, needy and starving. These situations are very real and people are suffering but do you ever see the good points of Africa being shown on TV or printed in the newspapers?' – Gabriella Gray, 14

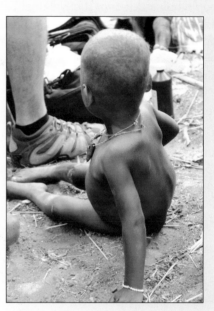

The Press

What people read in the newspapers can also influence how they think about other social groups, including ethnic and 'racial' minorities. If, for example, people from India are always presented as poor, starving or the victims of drought, that creates a false picture of Indians in general, even though it is right to report the human tragedies. Newspaper readers may never get to hear about the Indian scientists, writers, entrepreneurs, film-makers, artists, engineers and so on, not to mention the everyday, normal lives of normal people.

News reports

🔡 In groups

Discuss Sekai's and Gabriella's comments. Do you think the media stereotypes Africans?

Study some recent editions of either a national newspaper or a local newspaper. Discuss the reports and articles they carry about people from ethnic minorities. What images of them do they convey? Do they present a true picture of what their lives are like and the contribution they make to society?

For your file

What do you think newspapers should be doing to make sure that they do not reinforce stereotyping? Write an e-mail either to a national or local newspaper saying what you think the editor and staff should be doing to make sure that they do not stereotype people in their paper.

Gambling – the lure and the law

Gambling is one of the country's favourite leisure activities. Every week millions of people buy a ticket for the National Lottery and watch the draw on television. Other popular forms of gambling are betting on horse races, doing the football pools and going to bingo. There are an estimated 1 million regular online gamblers spending an average £1000 a year.

Officially, the law does not allow children to gamble. But many children do. Surveys suggest that 91% of under 18s had gambled at least once in their lives.

Why do young people gamble?

❝ It's glamorous. You see people in films and on TV gambling and you want to be like them. ❞

❝ It's fun. It gives you something to do when you're bored. ❞

❝ It's exciting. You're taking a risk and it gives you a real buzz waiting to see if you've won. ❞

❝ It's a way of escaping from the real world and all your problems. ❞

❝ The people I know who gamble do it because they can't stop themselves. They're addicted. ❞

❝ People gamble to try and win lots of money to make their dreams come true. ❞

Gambling and the law

There are tight legal restrictions on gambling. The laws are designed to enable people who choose to gamble to enjoy the pleasure of gambling, and at the same time to protect them from being cheated or exploited. For example, all fruit machines are required by law to return a minimum of 71 per cent of the stake money in prizes.

Young people are protected by making it illegal for them to gamble until they are considered old enough to gamble responsibly. The law says that you are not allowed to take part in most forms of gambling until you are 18. But you can do the football pools or buy a National Lottery ticket when you are 16, and you can play fruit machines with a token/cash payout at any age.

⚃ In groups

'It's too easy for young people to gamble. There sho be tighter controls.' Do you agree?

Discuss why gambling is condemned in some religio Make a list of all the moral and religious arguments against gambling you can think of, and say why you agree or disagree with them.

For your file

Write a statement saying what you think are the reasons why people gamble, what your attitude to gambling is and whether you think the gambling laws should be changed.

Winners and losers

A very few people who gamble win huge amounts of money, but most people who gamble lose their money. Because so many people gamble, the gambling industry is big business, with a vast daily turnover of more than £110 million.

The winners in the gambling industry are the people who make profits from the money that is gambled – for example, the pools companies and the bookmakers.

The other big winner is the government which receives over £1.7 billion a year in taxes on gambling.

Gambling – the odds

When you gamble, the odds are stacked against you. These are the approximate chances you have of winning in certain forms of gambling:

National Lottery draw	14 million to 1
Slot machines	600 to 1
Roulette	35 to 1
Scratchcards	5.5 to 1

Fruit Machine Facts

1 About 65% of teenagers play fruit machines. Of these, roughly 6% will become addicted to them.

2 Although fruit machines require a low cash input to start with, the rate the machines play at means money is used up very quickly. At least £3 is spent by addicts on each machine.

3 There's no skill at all involved in playing fruit machines, just as there's no surefire way to beat the system. Far more money goes into the machine than is paid out.

4 Never think of a fruit machine as an easy way to make money. You may have a couple of big wins when you begin playing, but don't let this fool you into putting more money in. Regardless of how many times you get lucky, you're in a no-win situation.

5 If you think you have a problem with fruit machines, speak to your parents. You may need professional help to break the habit. Don't forget you can always call Childline on 0800 1111.

The National Lottery

Since its introduction in November 1994, the National Lottery has proved a huge success. Around 70% of adults play on a regular basis.

The success of the National Lottery means that by July 2008 22 billion pounds had been distributed to 'good causes', such as sports and arts projects, funded by the National Lotteries charities board. The National Lottery will contribute almost £2.2 billion towards the funding for the London 2012 Olympic Games and Paralympic Games.

4.5p Running costs
0.5p Camelot / **12p** Government
28p Good causes
50p Prizes
5p Retailers

Where each pound spent on a lottery ticket goes

However, many charities reported that there was a significant fall in the amount of donations they received, following the introduction of the lottery. Critics also argue that it is wrong for the lottery to be run as a profit-making venture and that the licence to run the lottery in future should go to a non-profit-making organisation. They also say that the introduction of the lottery has led to the creation of a gambling culture, in which more people are interested in and addicted to gambling. In particular, it encourages lots of the poorest members of society to spend money they cannot afford on lottery tickets rather than essentials, such as food and clothing.

In groups

Talk about the National Lottery. What do you think of the criticisms that are made about the way it is run and the influence that it has had? Do you think introducing the National Lottery was a good idea? Do you think any changes should be made to the National Lottery? Give reasons for your views.

Teenage gambling

'Gambling has taken over my life!'

Two young people tell how gambling has affected their lives.

Keri

Keri (14) spends all her money on scratchcards, even though she's legally too young to buy them …

" The first time I bought a scratchcard I felt really nervous. But my friends were all doing it, and I didn't want to be the odd one out. I was sure the shopkeeper would know we were under-age. But he didn't say anything. We probably got away with it because we all look a bit older than we really are.

I only had a pound on me and I didn't win anything. But one of my friends did and I couldn't wait to have another go. I went back the next day and I won a tenner. It gave me such a great feeling. I bought a few more, but I didn't win again that day.

Then the following week, I had another win. I began to think I must be one of those people born lucky. Especially as none of my friends were winning. They began to lose interest and started saying it was a mug's game.

But the more cards I bought, the more convinced I became that one day I'd buy the one that would win me the jackpot. It got so that I couldn't walk past a newsagent's without wanting to go in and buy a scratchcard.

I love the thrill as you see the numbers being revealed and I'm just waiting for the day when I have that big win. I get some money for babysitting at weekends and it all goes on scratchcards.

Once I even took some money out of my mum's purse. I know I shouldn't have done, but I was going to put it back when I won. Only that day I lost.

My best friend keeps telling me that I'm obsessed. We fell out yesterday because she says I'm boring. She says I've never got any money to do anything and all I think about is scratchcards. I'm frightened I'm going to lose her friendship. But it's got so I don't think I can live without doing them. **"**

Jason

Jason is 15 and addicted to arcade machines. He's stolen things from his home and sold them to fund his habit …

" When I was 12, I started to hang round with this older boy, Kev. He took me down the arcades and taught me how to play the machines. I found it really exciting, especially the noise and the lights flashing when you won.

Before I knew it I was hooked. I couldn't wait to get down the arcade. I started skipping school to go there and I'd spend all my dinner money and pocket money on the machines.

I was so desperate for money that I raided my savings and when they ran out I started to sell my things. I even stole my sister's personal stereo and sold it to get money for the machines.

The breaking point came when I started shoplifting. Of course, I got caught and when my parents found out they went berserk.

But they've been really supportive. They've made me realise that I'm addicted to gambling in the way that some people get addicted to drugs. Stopping going down the arcade to play the machines has been really difficult. I've suffered from withdrawal symptoms. I go to see this counsellor and he's really helpful. He's made me face up to the fact that I've got a problem. **"**

🔘 In groups

Discuss the effect that gambling has had on Keri's life and Jason's life. Talk about why some people get addicted to buying scratchcards or playing arcade machines.

Problem gambling

Experts consider that a person has a problem with gambling when:

✦ They are unable to stop gambling whether they are winning or losing.

✦ The urge to gamble overrides all other considerations.

✦ They are psychologically dependent on gambling because they experience a 'high' when they are gambling.

If you think a friend has a gambling problem, you can help them by:

1 Letting them know by saying you think they may have a problem.

2 Suggesting that they need to be honest with themselves and others.

3 Encouraging them to talk to their parents and/or a trusted adult.

Who can help?

✦ GamCare: website GamCare.org.uk

✦ GamCare helpline: 0845 6000 133

Responsible gambling

Gambling can quickly get out of control and create serious problems with money, relationships and other aspects of your life. In order to prevent problems occurring, when you gamble remember the following points:

✦ You are buying entertainment – not investing your money.

✦ Before playing, set strict limits on how much time and money you are going to spend.

✦ Quit when you are ahead.

✦ Only gamble with money you can afford to lose.

✦ Do not 'chase' your losses.

✦ Keep up your other interests and hobbies to ensure your gambling does not take over.

✦ Gambling in moderation is okay and 'healthy'.

✦ The key is to gamble responsibly.

Role play

Role play the following scenes:

1 A group of friends are discussing what to do. Two of them want to go to an amusement arcade to play the machines and try to put pressure on the other two to go with them. Take it in turns to be the two who don't want to go, and discuss ways of saying no firmly.

2 A gang of friends are planning to pool their money to buy some scratchcards and to share any winnings. One of the friends is against the idea and thinks they'd get more value for money if they went to the swimming pool or the fairground instead. Take it in turns to be the 'odd one out'.

In groups

Discuss these statements and say whether you agree with them:

❝ *Only people who haven't got enough to do waste their time and money gambling.* ❞

❝ *Gambling creates more hardship and misery than it gives pleasure.* ❞

For your file

Write an article for a magazine for young people about teenage gambling, describing the problems that it can cause and offering advice on how to gamble responsibly.

What influences how you behave?

The way you behave is influenced by what your beliefs and values are. For example, in some situations your behaviour might depend on how important you think it is to impress people, compared to doing what you believe to be right.

What plays the most important part in influencing how you behave? Here are some possibilities. On your own, rank them in level of importance on a five-point scale – 1 for extremely important, 5 for not at all important.

Trying to avoid arguments

Standing up for what you believe is right

Making sure your actions don't hurt other people

Trying to impress people

Listening to what your parents and teachers say

Keeping out of trouble

Doing what your religion says you should do

Keeping your temper

Following the latest fashion

Behaving with courtesy

Telling the truth

Looking after your own interests

Imitating the behaviour of your idols

Respecting other people's opinions and beliefs

Keeping your promises

Doing what your friends want you to do

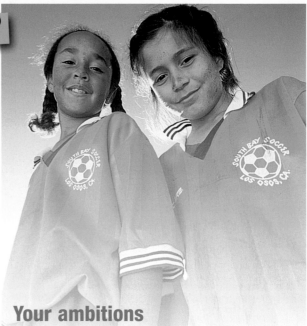

Your ambitions

What you believe to be important, and what your values are, will influence your ambitions.

Here is what a group of young people said when asked what their ambitions were:

" To make money. "

" To get married. "

" To have a satisfying career. "

" To live a long life. "

" To contribute to the community. "

" To have people's respect. "

" To travel the world. "

" To become famous. "

" To make the most of my talents. "

" To have children. "

" To help other people. "

" To be happy. "

" To keep fit and healthy. "

In groups

Compare how you have ranked the things that influence your behaviour and discuss what you think the most important influences should be.

In groups

Study the list of things which young people said were important to them when asked to think about their ambitions. Add anything else to the list which you think is important. Then each list what are the five most important things to you personally and talk about why they are important to you.

Heroes and idols

Discuss what Derek Stuart says in his article about the difference between idols and heroes. Do you agree with him? What do you think is the difference between an idol and a hero? Together decide what your definition of a hero is.

Draw up a list of people you consider to be heroes who your group would put in their 'hall of fame'. Draft a short statement explaining your reasons for including each person. Then present your views in a class discussion and agree on a class list of our top twenty heroes.

Someone I admire

Think of someone you know personally and admire for some reason, perhaps because of what they have achieved, the way they behave towards other people or the courage and determination they have shown in difficult circumstances. It could be a relative, a friend of the family or a neighbour.

Study the list of qualities (below) and pick out the qualities which make you admire them:

> *intelligence   tact   courage
> determination   unselfishness
> tolerance   cheerfulness   patience
> generosity   loyalty   reliability
> kindness   sympathy   creativity*

Take it in turns to tell each other about the person you admire and why you admire them.

Idols or heroes?

by Derek Stuart

Everyone has famous people that they look up to and admire, but are they idols or heroes?

Many teenagers when asked who they admire most give the name of a film star, a pop singer, a TV celebrity or a sports star. These people certainly have talent and are often good-looking. Many of them have worked hard and shown determination to achieve what they have. They are rich and famous and have exciting lifestyles. But are they really heroes?

The way I see it, a hero is somebody who has shown exceptional qualities. They are people like Nelson Mandela, who was prepared to go to prison to fight for his rights. They are people who are prepared to risk or sacrifice their lives for other people. They are people who achieve things against the odds and who set an example to us all by the way they behave.

So when I'm drawing up my list of heroes for my hall of fame, I'm looking beyond the stars of stage and screen, playing field and catwalk to those exceptional human beings whose behaviour has been truly heroic.

Cause for concern

The eight reports on these two pages all appeared in the Daily Mail on Saturday 27 September 2008. Which of the issues raised in the reports do you think is the most important?

A

For the first time, the married are the minority

By Steve Doughty Social Affairs Correspondent

The number of married couples has dropped to fewer than half the adult population for the first time since records began.

Government figures show there were 21,535,000 married adults in England and Wales in 2006 – just 49.5 per cent of the population over 16.

The count, which was released by the Office of National Statistics, also reveals that, for millions of young people, being married is now a minority lifestyle.

The number of those in their teens and twenties who are married has dropped below a million, with more than nine in ten aged under thirty choosing to cohabit or remain single.

B

Jobs Gloom Hits the Shops

Thousands of bank and shop jobs are under threat after high street giants yesterday began announcing the first in a series of redundancies.

HSBC said it is to cut 500 jobs in the UK as part of a global reduction of 1,100, following Bradford and Bingley's announcement earlier in the week that they are to axe 370 jobs.

High street stores are also reducing their workforce amid a collapse in consumer spending.

Yesterday the curtains and furnishings firm Rosebys, which employs 2,000 staff, went into administration, while JJB Sports and John Lewis revealed alarming trading figures.

C

Smokers to be confronted with horror pictures

Graphic images hammering home the dangers of smoking will appear on cigarette packets from next week.

The pictures will include a throat tumour engorged with blood, a corpse in a morgue and a baby in an incubator.

Sir Liam Donaldson, the Government's chief medical officer, said the images show the 'grim reality' of smoking.

Despite almost two million smokers quitting in the last decade, the habit is still the biggest killer in England, causing 87,000 early deaths a year.

D

Toxic peril of powdered ecstasy

By Matthew Hickley Home Affairs Correspondent

Drug experts have warned of a 'worrying' new danger from Ecstasy being sold in a highly concentrated powder form.

Users are increasingly buying the illegal rave drug –which kills around 50 people a year – as a white powder because dealers have begun selling the more familiar tablets at a weaker strength.

But clubbers often have no idea what they are buying and doctors say a growing number are arriving in hospital having snorted Ecstasy after mistaking it for cocaine, not realising that Ecstasy powder is ten times as toxic.

E

Gun police storm jet on runway to grab 'terror' pair

From Allan Hall in Berlin

SAS-trained German commandos stormed an airliner yesterday to seize two suspects they believed were plotting a terrorist outrage.

The armed Special Action Commandos grabbed a 23-year-old Somalian and a 24-year-old German born in Somalia, from the KLM aircraft at Cologne without shots being fired.

German prosecutors said both were suspected members of the Islamic Jihad Union and had tickets to travel on to Pakistan from Amsterdam via Uganda.

Speculation in Germany was that police believed they were going to Pakistan to receive further terrorist training – or possibly orders for attacks on U.S. bases in the country.

Review of the sports we see free on TV

The list of sporting events which must be broadcast free-to-air is being reviewed by the Government.

Highlights of England World Cup qualifying games could be added to protected events such as Wimbledon and the Olympics.

The decision comes after millions missed out on seeing highlights of England football games against Andorra and Croatia.

The Irish cable channel Setanta, which owned the broadcasting rights to away games, could not agree a deal with a terrestrial channel for a highlights package.

F

G

Teenage boy knifed to death yards from a police station

Daily Mail Reporter

A teenager attacked just yards from a police station has become the 27th youngster to be stabbed to death in London this year.

Craig Steven Marshall, 19, died yesterday morning after being knifed outside a block of flats in Acton, West London.

He managed to stagger to nearby Acton police station, but collapsed at the counter. Witnesses said he was covered in blood.

He died of his injuries at 8am.

Residents of the flats said the stabbing may have been related to an ongoing feud which started over a drug deal.

In pairs

Study the reports and then list them in order of what you consider to be the importance of the issues they raise. For example, if you think D is the most important write down 1–D and so on.

In groups

Compare your lists. Talk about why you consider some issues to be more important than others.

Imagine your group is the editorial committee of a weekly TV news programme in which topical issues are discussed. Decide which four issues you would include in the programme. Then role play a discussion about one of the issues.

H

Cherry juice 'is as good as 23 portions of fruit and veg'

Drinking a glass of cherry juice a day offers the same health benefits as eating 23 portions of fruit and vegetables, research reveals.

It found 250ml of the juice contained more antioxidants than five portions of peas, tomatoes, water melon, carrots and banana.

Previous research has shown that antioxidants – which target harmful molecules in the body called free radicals – can help prevent cancer, heart disease, stroke and ageing.

For your file

Choose one of the issues on which you have a strong opinion and write a letter expressing your views on the issue.

Cut out a newspaper report which raises an issue that you feel strongly about. Put it in your file and write a comment saying why you have chosen that particular report.

Separation and divorce

Dealing with divorce

Marie (14), Ellen (12) and Laura (10) have watched their parents get divorced. They talk about what they have learned from their experience.

Why do people get divorced?

Laura: Because they don't like each other as much as they did before.

Ellen: They are changing or have changed.

Marie: Each situation is unique and has its own set of reasons. Most reasons are too complicated and adult-related for parents to share with their children. That's good. There are some things we really don't need to know. Don't be afraid to say that to a parent who is telling you things about the other parent that you think are none of your business (but say it nicely!).

I'm scared about my parents' divorce. What can I do?

Laura: It's okay to be scared. I was scared when my parents got divorced. Just hang on in there!

Ellen: Your parents aren't spending as much time with you and they might be cranky. That doesn't mean they don't love you. They need some space and some time.

Marie: Of course, you're scared – it's a scary thing. Think about why you are scared. Let your parents know what you are thinking. They can reassure you. They're scared too, but you can all support each other.

Can I make my parents get back together?

Laura: No, and don't try. If they stay together, they won't be happy and they'll probably just fight.

Ellen: No. Lots of kids probably try, but it won't work, so don't get involved doing something that will just frustrate everyone.

Marie: Just like us, our parents have to choose their own paths. You can't do anything that will get them back together. It's their problem and their job to make life work for themselves. The decision to divorce is probably not something they made in a hurry. They've likely thought about all of the possibilities and they see this as the best thing to do.

Is it my fault that my parents are getting divorced?

Laura: No. How could it be? They're the grown-ups, you're just a kid.

Ellen: No. This is between your parents. There's nothing a kid could do that would cause a divorce.

 In groups

Discuss what Marie, Ellen and Laura say about parents divorcing, and say whether or not you agree with them.

List all the different reasons you can think of why relationships between parents break up. Is it none of your business, or do you think children have a right to an explanation when their parents decide to split up? Does it depend on how old you are?

? What do you think?

In groups, study each of the eight statements below. On your own write down whether you agree with it (A), disagree with it (D) or are not sure (N/S). Then compare your views in a group discussion.

1 It's better for parents to split up than to stay together for their children's sake.

2 Splitting up is an easy option. Too many parents take the easy way out.

3 Children should never take one parent's side.

4 It's better for parents to split up than to spend all the time arguing and quarrelling.

5 Parents should involve children in discussions about splitting up.

6 A one-parent family can never be as happy as a two-parent family.

7 Parents who split up are selfish. They're only thinking of themselves.

8 Children are bound to suffer when parents split up.

A mixture of feelings

Children often experience a mixture of feelings when their parents separate.

Whatever you feel, it's important to recognise your feelings and not to bottle them up. Talking can help. So find someone you can trust and talk to them honestly.

Who decides who you live with?

In the majority of divorce cases, it's your parents who will decide which of them you are going to live with. They will also agree the arrangements for you to see your other parent. But if they are unable to agree, then the court will decide.

The court will take your views into consideration as well as those of your parents. The court may make two orders – a **residence order** and a **contact order**.

A residence order states which person you are going to live with. A contact order specifies the arrangements for you to see your absent parent. A typical arrangement is that you will spend alternate weekends with them and a week with them at Christmas, Easter and in the summer.

In pairs

'Children should always have the final say in deciding who they are going to live with.' Discuss this view.

Shock

❝ I just couldn't believe it. I felt totally numb. I went round in a kind of daze. It wasn't until my grandma talked to me that I realised I'd been suffering from shock.❞ Nathan (14)

Anger

❝ I was furious with them both. I started taking it out on everybody and everything. I played truant from school and even got in trouble with the police. Of course, that just made things worse. ❞ Darrell (15)

Sadness

❝ I felt so unhappy. I just couldn't stop crying. We'd been such a happy family and now it was all over. ❞ Heather (13)

Guilt

❝ I got myself into a right state. I was convinced that I must be to blame. ❞ Alanna (14)

Relief

❝ To be honest, it was a relief. The tension had become so unbearable that I'd dread going home to find them fighting again. Now there was an end in sight. ❞ Mitchell (16)

Insecurity

❝ I felt frightened and insecure. I didn't know what was going to happen to me. Would we have enough money? Would I have to change schools? What would my friends think? ❞ Kirsten (14)

For your file

Study Pat's letter (below) and write an answer to it.

My parents are separating and I feel it's all my fault. Whenever they argue it seems to be about me. Mum says Dad's too hard on me and he says I'm selfish and spoilt. I feel desperate. I'd do anything to help keep them together. I couldn't bear it if they split up. – Pat

Coping with change

When your parents separate there can be major changes in your life. You may have to move home or school. The parent you live with may be short of money. You may find it hard to keep contact with the absent parent. You may find it difficult when the parent you live with starts to form a new relationship.

In groups

Read the stories on this page and talk about the changes that these people had to face when their parents separated.

1 Talk about what it feels like to become part of a one-parent family after being in a two-parent family. How typical do you think Barbara's experience is?

2 Discuss Chris's problem and say what you think he should do about it.

3 Talk about what Xanthe says. Do you think her experience is unusual? Explain why.

A quarter of all teenagers whose parents divorce lose contact with the absent parent after two years. Discuss why you think this happens. How important do you think it is to try to keep in contact with both your parents after a divorce? Is it always desirable, whatever the circumstances? Give reasons for your views.

In pairs

Many children find it difficult to tell their friends and other people that their parents are separating. Discuss why they find it hard. Is it better to be upfront about it and to tell everybody, or do you think it's your family's business and that there's no need to tell anyone if you don't feel like it?

We had to move to a small flat

Barbara lived in a large house before her parents split up, but it has now been sold and Barbara is living in a small flat with her mother.

'It's not nearly as nice as our old place. She says it's only until she can get on her feet, and then we'll get a better place.

Also, she has to work full-time now. She's always tired – she comes in, does a few jobs around the flat and then collapses in front of the TV.'

I want to be with my mates

Chris found that it was a problem pleasing both his father and himself. He felt really guilty because he was bored when he was with his dad.

'I spend every weekend with my dad. We really get on and I know he enjoys my visits. The trouble is, I end up feeling really bored. Dad makes me feel guilty because on a Saturday night I want to go out with my mates, not sit at home and watch TV, however much he likes having me around.'

I get the best of both worlds

Some young people, like Xanthe, speak positively of an arrangement where they split their time between two parents.

'I actually enjoyed seeing my parents separately. We often used to find it difficult to agree on things, but now I do different things with my mum and with my dad. They make more of an effort to do things with me, like taking me ice-skating or to the cinema, and I make less of a fuss when they ask me to help out with chores and things like that. I feel I get the best of both worlds.

I also spend more time with each of them on their own, and have got closer to them and know them better as people. Now that we have adjusted to life after the break-up, I actually prefer it like this to how it was before.'

Living in a stepfamily

❝ I hated my stepmum, Sharon, but now I know her better, I think she's really sweet and nice. We disagree sometimes and she aggravates me a lot, but she's OK really. ❞ Janet (14)

❝ When I visited dad, it was fun having a stepbrother to do things with, but my father wasn't there for me. He showed favouritism to my stepbrother. He spent more time with him than me. I really felt pushed into the background. ❞
Jason (16)

❝ I was gob-smacked when Mum told us she was pregnant. So were my stepbrothers. We were pretty mean to Mum during her pregnancy. Amazingly when Pete was born, it brought us together because he belonged to both families. ❞
Rachel (16)

88 In groups

What do you learn from the statements above about the problems children face when settling in to a stepfamily? What other problems and difficulties might stepchildren face?

Study the article (right). Which do you think is the most useful piece of advice **a)** on how to cope with step-parents; **b)** on how to get on with stepbrothers and stepsisters?

How to cope with **step-parents**

If you're going to be living with your step-parents, don't expect everything to be brilliant from the start. Everyone will have a lot of adjusting to do, and just getting used to each other's habits is a big step.

Your step-parent isn't a substitute for your real mum or dad. But that doesn't mean you can't form a close, loving relationship with him or her. Why not give it a chance?

If you do have problems with a step-parent, it can help to talk to someone who isn't closely involved, maybe a friend or a teacher you get on with. Often someone a bit more distant from the problem can stand back, take a good look and suggest things that might help.

Try to get to know your stepmum or dad as a person, not just see them as a threat. Until you actually find out a bit about him or her and discover what their personality's like, how do you know you aren't going to get on?

If you really are having big problems with a step-parent, try having a private word with your mum or dad about it. They're still your mum or dad and will want to sort things out.

Brothers and sisters

Adjusting to having a stepbrother or stepsister also takes time. If you're having problems, think of the following:

All families are different. So if, for example, you're used to having a lie-in at weekends and your stepbrothers and sisters like to get up at the crack of dawn and watch TV with the sound up high, you'll need to reach a compromise. Of course, that means talking about how you feel – not shouting!

If you do argue, it's not the end of the world. After all, real brothers and sisters argue all the time, so it's only natural to argue with your new brothers and sisters, isn't it?

Try to see stepbrothers and sisters as potential friends. If you both make an effort, you can end up close and good mates – much better than being at war with them!

Respect their space and privacy. Even if you have to share a room, work out a few ground rules between you so there aren't any misunderstandings.

Your mum or dad remarrying definitely takes a lot of getting used to and can be a very upsetting time. But if everyone makes the effort, you should end up as a happy family – it just takes a bit of effort and a lot of compromise all round.

For your file

A friend called Jan is very upset because her mother is getting remarried. She is feeling resentful and anxious about moving in with her stepfather and his two children. She thinks she will have to share a bedroom. Write a letter offering Jan advice on how to cope with the new situation.

Safety at home

Every year thousands of people are injured in accidents at home. You need to know what to do in an emergency. The commonest type of accidents are falls.

+ First aid for cuts

If you lose too much blood your body won't get enough oxygen. Severe bleeding can cause death, so the first thing you must do is stop the bleeding. Put your thumb and/or fingers on the wound and press firmly. If it is a large cut, try pressing the edges together. Keep pressing until the bleeding stops. This may take up to 15 minutes.

If direct pressure won't stop the bleeding, press gently but firmly above and below the wound. If you can, raise the injured part so that it is above the level of the casualty's chest. This slows down the blood flow from the heart to the injured part.

A large cut which won't stop bleeding or which has gaping edges may need stitches. Don't try to clean it or to take out any object embedded in the wound. Removing it could cause more damage and might increase the bleeding, since the object may be plugging the wound. Bandage the wound with a clean dressing and get medical help.

If it is a small cut or a graze, clean the wound with soap and water, then dry it and put on a sterile dressing or an adhesive plaster. The size of the pad touching the wound must always be larger than the wound. Don't use any creams or ointments. They do not help and may delay healing by making the skin soggy.

+ What to do if someone falls

- Even if you think a bone is broken, do not move the person if the injury looks serious. This is particularly important if you think the neck or spine is injured because damage to the spinal cord can cause permanent paralysis.
- Go and call an ambulance.
- Keep the person warm.
- Do not give the injured person anything to drink in case they need to be given an anaesthetic later.

+ First aid for fractures

Sometimes it may be difficult to tell for certain whether a bone is broken. Signs are as follows:
- pain and tenderness at the point of injury;
- swelling;
- deformity or unusual shape;
- loss of movement.

Do not move the casualty until you have immobilised the fracture, which means making sure it cannot move. Movement of the broken ends can cause more damage, pain and shock. If it is a broken leg, immobilise it by putting some soft padding between the legs and tying the injured leg gently but firmly to the other leg at the ankles and knees. If it is a broken arm, immobilise it by putting the casualty's arm across the chest and supporting it with an arm sling.

In pairs

Study the information on this page, then write answers to these questions.

1 What signs and symptoms may indicate that a casualty might have a fractured leg?

2 Explain the first aid treatment that you would give someone you suspect has
a) a broken leg, **b)** a broken arm.

3 If someone is bleeding badly, why is it dangerous? How would you try to stop the bleeding?

4 How would you treat **a)** a wound with an object embedded in it, **b)** a grazed knee?

For your file

Find out what you should do if someone is suffocating or choking, then write out a set of first aid instructions. Call them 'What to do if someone is suffocating' and 'What to do if someone is choking'.

✚ First aid for burns and scalds

When you get a burn or a scald, it damages your skin and destroys the blood vessels just below the surface. The first aid treatment is the same for burns and scalds.

1 Pour water over the burn at once. This reduces the heat in the skin.

2 Keep putting on cold water for at least ten minutes. Either hold the burn under a cold tap or dip it into a bowl or a bath of cold water.

3 Burnt skin often swells up. Take off anything near the burn which may be tight, such as a ring, a bracelet or a watch.

4 Cover the burn with a clean dry dressing from your first aid box or use a cotton pillow case or a linen tea towel. This will help to protect the skin from the risk of infection.

5 If the person is badly burned, call an ambulance.

6 Don't try to pull off any clothes that are stuck to the skin. Don't put any cream or ointment on the burn or use a fluffy cloth to cover the burn.

🔘 In pairs

Discuss how scalding accidents can occur **a)** in the kitchen, **b)** in the bathroom. What steps can you take to try to prevent them occurring?

▷◁ Role play

Imagine one of you was baby-sitting when a young child got burned. Tell a friend how you gave the child first aid.

What to do if the house is on fire

1 Get everyone out of the house as fast as possible. Lots of deaths in fires are caused by people breathing in fumes and suffocating. So don't stay in the house and try to put the fire out.

2 Call the fire brigade by dialling 999. Don't just think that someone else will already have done so.

3 If you have time, close all doors and windows. This can stop the fire spreading, because it reduces draughts which may fan the flames.

If someone's clothes are on fire ...

▲ Pull the person to the ground. This stops the fire from spreading upwards towards the face.

▲ Grab a coat, rug or blanket and use it to smother the flames. But don't use anything made of nylon, because nylon shrivels and melts in heat.

Many potential fire hazards are found in people's homes

Chip pans

Many kitchen fires are caused by chip pans catching fire, often because the pan is too full. If a chip pan catches fire, switch the cooker off, cover the pan with a lid or damp cloth and leave it to cool down. Do not take it off the cooker and put it under the cold tap.

For your file

Design a poster *either* to tell people how to protect their homes from fire *or* to tell them what action to take in an emergency if a house catches fire or if someone is burned.

What is child abuse?

Abuse occurs when adults hurt children or young people under 18, either physically or in some other way. Usually the adult is someone the child or young person knows well, such as a parent, relative or friend of the family.

There are four main kinds of abuse:

Physical abuse includes hitting, kicking and punching, and may even lead to death.
Emotional abuse includes sarcasm, degrading punishments, threats and not giving love and affection, which can undermine a young person's confidence.
Neglect occurs when basic needs, such as food, warmth and medical care, are not met. Being thrown out of home may also be an example of neglect.

Sexual abuse occurs if an adult pressurises or forces a young person to take part in any kind of sexual activity. This can include kissing, touching the young person's genitals or breasts, intercourse or oral sex. If an adult asks you to touch his or her genitals, or to look at pornographic magazines or videos, these are examples of sexual abuse.

As well as causing suffering at the time, there may be long-term difficulties for young people who have been abused. All forms of abuse are wrong and have damaging effects on children and young people.

No one knows exactly why some adults take advantage of their position of authority over young people in this way. There may be many different reasons. Stress, money problems, unhappy circumstances, the feeling of having no power in adult relationships, and having been abused as a child may all play a part. But it is hard to predict with certainty which factors cause an adult to abuse a child.

Some adults may even convince themselves that there is nothing wrong with their behaviour, or that it is for the child's own good.

But whatever the reason, abuse is **always** wrong and it is **never** the young person's fault.

But Nina's got a new pair! It's not fair!

*Not getting your own way all the time is **not** an example of child abuse.*

 In groups

'A good hiding never did anyone any harm.'
Say why you agree or disagree with this view.

FACTS and FICTIONS about ABUSE

1 When a young person is abused, the offender is more likely to be a stranger.
FALSE – *In the majority of reported cases the offender is someone the young person knows.*

2 Girls are more at risk of abuse than boys.
FALSE – *Boys are at risk almost as much as girls, though boys report abuse less.*

3 The majority of offences of abuse are carried out by men.
TRUE – *Most reported cases of abuse are by men.*

4 Victims are sometimes to blame for the abuse because of the way they behaved.
FALSE – *It is never the victim's fault, no matter how they behaved. It is always the abuser's fault.*

5 If anyone attempts to touch you in a way that makes you feel uncomfortable, you have the right to tell them not to do so.
TRUE – *It is your body and you have the right to decide who touches you and who doesn't.*

Sexual abuse

I feel so guilty and ashamed

There was this friend of my dad's who I got on really well with. One evening he came round while my parents were out and put this video on which showed people having sex. He sat down beside me and put his arm round me and started touching me all over. I tried to tell him to stop but he wouldn't listen and made me touch him. He told me that what we were doing was all right and it was to be our secret. I've never told anyone about it before, because I feel so guilty and ashamed about what happened.

Kayleigh

If you are being abused, it is extremely important to understand that *you* haven't done anything wrong. The victim is *never* to blame for what happens to them, and yet so many victims of abuse feel guilty. No one deserves to be abused, and no matter how you react in a situation where you're being abused (whether you don't put up a fight, whether you maybe even experience sexual feelings that aren't entirely unpleasant) you are not responsible for what happened to you. If you have feelings of guilt, try to fight them, because you have *nothing* to feel guilty about. Concentrate on feeling angry with your abuser instead, and determined to protect yourself and put things right.

The most important thing to do if you have been abused is to tell someone about it. Choose a responsible adult who you trust. If you're afraid to tell a parent or guardian (perhaps because the abuser is someone close to them), choose another older relative, a teacher you like or your doctor. If you can't think of anyone you'd feel comfortable talking to, or you think you might prefer to talk to someone you don't know, you can get help and advice by ringing a helpline.

NSPCC Child Protection Helpline: this is a free 24-hour service, which you can ring either if you think you are being abused yourself, or if you are worried about a friend. Telephone: 0800 800 500.

Childline: this is a helpline for young people who are in trouble or danger. You can also contact them if you are concerned about a friend being abused. Telephone: 0800 1111.

What happens next?

When you tell an adult about serious abuse, he or she may have to involve other people to help you sort things out. Usually there will be a social worker, and sometimes a police officer and doctor. What happens next is called an **investigation**. In order to help you, these professionals will ask you questions to find out exactly what happened. These questions may be embarrassing or difficult. But the adults involved are used to talking to young people who have had similar experiences, and should make it as easy as possible for you. As part of the investigation, the professionals will probably also speak to your family and other people who know you well. After the investigation there may be a **case conference** where the professionals will meet and make decisions about how best to help you. You might be able to go along to all or part of the case conference.

During the investigation and case conference, it is important that you make sure that the professionals know how *you* feel. Try not to be afraid to ask questions, and let them know how they could make things easier for you.

Young people who have been abused are only taken away from home if it is felt that it is dangerous for them to stay. The majority stay in their own home. Most of those who are removed return home just as soon as it is felt that they will be safe.

Saying no

If an adult starts pressurising you to do something you don't want to do, tell them firmly to stop.

With your partner, take it in turns to practise saying no. Role play a scene in which a friend is putting pressure on you to do something that is reckless or dangerous. Practise saying no politely but firmly.

33

Safety in the street

We would all like to be able to walk through the streets alone without feeling frightened, and we all have a right to be able to feel safe whatever we do.

Unfortunately, sometimes that is not always possible so it is important to know what we can do to make sure that we stay safe.

Staying safe in the street...

- Keep to main, well-lit paths.
- Don't walk closely behind people who are walking alone.
- Don't accept unorganised lifts.
- Invest in a personal alarm.
- Walk facing the traffic. Think about the clothes you are wearing if you have to walk home late at night. For example, trousers are better than tight skirts.
- If attacked shout FIRE – not 'rape' or 'help', as more people are likely to respond.
- Make sure that your mobile phone is charged.
- Be aware of your surroundings – especially at a cash point, telephone booth, near pubs and clubs.
- Tell someone where you are going and when you will be back.

Safety on buses...

- If you're waiting at a quiet bus stop at night, look to see if there's a café or shop that you can wait inside till your bus comes.
- At night don't go upstairs on a double-decker. Try to find an aisle seat and sit near the driver.
- Don't travel alone if you can avoid doing so.
- If you feel threatened go and stand close to the driver and tell them why you are doing so.
- If you are getting off alone at a quiet stop, arrange for someone to meet you there.

What should you do if ...

Discuss what you think a person should do in each of these situations.

1 You are travelling home on the bus late at night and a stranger comes and sits next to you and starts to chat you up.

2 You are walking along the street and a car pulls up alongside and the people inside offer you a lift.

3 You are travelling on a crowded bus and you feel someone stroking your thigh.

4 You are walking through a shopping precinct and you get the feeling that someone is following you.

5 You are walking past a group of people and they start shouting insults and making lewd comments.

6 You enter the hallway of the block of flats where you live and you see someone hanging about that you don't like the look of.

7 You are walking home with a friend who suggests that you take a short cut that will save you twenty minutes but it means going down a lonely lane.

8 The person who said they'd drive you home has taken drugs or got drunk and you've no money to get yourself home.

Safety in public places

If you like to hang around in parks, on the beach, in arcades, fast food places, shopping precincts, or any other public place, take these precautions:

- Stay with your friends, or at least within sight of them.
- Avoid these places at night, especially if they are deserted or tend to attract gangs.
- Avoid deserted toilets. Go with a friend.

Keep an eye out for lone adults, especially men or older boys, who hang about where young people congregate. If he tries to make friends with you, or he offers you money, food, drink or drugs, refuse and act cold or distant. If he persists or you see him playing a lot with a particular child, tell the shopkeepers in the arcade, your parents or another trusted adult about him.

If someone talks to you persistently

'I was stuck on a train once during a breakdown, and this middle-aged man started chatting to me. I didn't like him because he was pushy, so I acted cold and moved away from him. He got the message, but then he turned to this other teenage girl and started talking to her. She was too embarrassed to be rude to him, and pretty soon he was touching her earrings and necklace and asking her about her boyfriends and making her blush. She looked embarrassed because everyone could hear.'

Don't let someone intimidate you into putting up with pushy, personal, or unpleasant conversation. If he's insensitive enough to keep bothering you, you don't have to worry about being rude to him. If brief, cold answers and a turned-away head don't stop him, pointedly moving away from him should. If you are absolutely stuck next to him in a rush-hour crowd, shout, 'There's a man bothering me here, please let me through.' Make sure he's the one who is embarrassed, not you.

The Golden Rule of Self-Defence

The golden rule of self-defence is to pay attention to and trust your instincts. Countless victims of sexual assault and other crimes have said, 'I felt something was wrong, but I didn't want to look stupid, so I didn't do anything.' If you feel uncomfortable around a person or a place, if a warning signal goes off somewhere deep inside you, if you feel scared or just uneasy, don't ignore it. It is always better to act on your warning instincts and never know whether you were right than to ignore them and find yourself a victim; a moment of looking foolish is nothing compared to being assaulted.

In groups

Plan a short video for young people designed to tell them how to stay safe in the street. First, decide exactly what tips you want your video to give, then discuss how you are going to put your messages across. Draft a detailed plan for your video, then choose someone to explain it to the rest of the class and share your ideas in a class discussion.

For your file

Design a leaflet for young people called 'Safety in the Street – How to Protect Yourself Outside'.

Safety in the street

Every year thousands of young people are injured on the roads. There is more risk of a cyclist having a road accident than any other road user except a motorcyclist.

Cycling Safely

You are most at risk on a bicycle when you are either turning right, going round a roundabout, crossing the pavement or riding at night.

Turning right

When you're turning right, look behind you for traffic. If it's clear, give an arm signal early. Then move towards the centre of the road to take up the correct position for turning. Repeat the arm signal and give a last 'life-saver' look over your right shoulder before turning.

At roundabouts

You have to give way to traffic coming from the right. It is usually safer to stay in the left-hand lane all the way round. But you need to watch out for vehicles wanting to cross your path to leave the roundabout.

Crossing the pavement

Lots of accidents are caused by children riding across the pavement and straight out into the road. You should wheel your bicycle across the pavement and then wait for a gap in the traffic.

At night

Riding at night is dangerous because it can be difficult for drivers to see you. It is against the law to ride without lights and a reflector. It is also a good idea to wear something bright which reflects in a car's headlights. Another thing you can do is to fix reflectors on the pedals.

In groups

1 The most dangerous age for cyclists is 12 to 14, and five times as many boys get hurt as girls. Discuss why.

2 List the various ways of carrying things on a bicycle. Which are the safest ways and why?

3 'It should be illegal to ride a bicycle when you're not wearing a safety helmet.' Say why you agree or disagree with this view.

4 Draw up a list of 'Dos' and 'Don'ts' for cyclists. Compare your list with the 'Extra Rules for Cyclists' in the Highway Code.

5 How often should you check your bicycle? Which parts should you check? Draft a bicycle maintenance checklist.

6 Prepare an outline for a TV advert designed to make young people of your age aware of the dangers of riding recklessly.

For your file

Study the information on this page. Design a comic strip or write a cautionary tale about a young person who gets hurt in a cycling accident because they weren't cycling safely.

Emergency first aid

When you are faced with an emergency, do not rush in immediately with first aid. Pause to assess the situation first. Look around to make sure that you are not going to endanger yourself or the casualty. You must then decide how the injury should be treated.

Shock

A person who has had a serious injury, severe pain or serious loss of blood may be suffering from the condition called shock. The symptoms of shock vary depending on how serious the condition is. The symptoms include paleness, feeling faint, cold and clammy skin, a weak and fast pulse, fast and shallow breathing. Shock can cause unconsciousness and even death. The aim of first aid for shock is to prevent the shock from getting worse.

1 Get the casualty to lie down and deal with any injuries.

2 If the casualty has lost a lot of blood, keep the head down and if possible raise the lower limbs. But do not do this if you think there may be a head injury or that a leg may be broken.

3 Cover the casualty with a blanket, rug or coat to keep him or her warm, but not too hot.

4 Do not give anything to drink in case the person needs to have an anaesthetic when she/he gets to hospital.

Unconsciousness

1 Check that the person is breathing properly. Make sure there are no obstructions in the mouth. Remove any false teeth, chewing gum or vomit.

2 Stop any severe bleeding by pressing firmly on the wound.

3 If the person stops breathing, give them mouth-to-mouth resuscitation immediately.

4 It can be dangerous for an unconscious person to lie on her or his back, because the tongue may fall back and block the airway. Once you are sure that breathing is satisfactory and any severe bleeding is controlled you should put the person in the recovery position (see diagram). This prevents the tongue from falling back and allows any blood, fluid or vomit to drain out of the mouth.

5 It can be dangerous to move someone who has broken bones or internal injuries. Do not move such a casualty unless you have to do so because there is further danger, such as from traffic or fire.

6 Do not leave an unconscious person alone unless you have to because there is no one else around and you need to fetch help.

1 Loosen tight clothing and remove glasses.

2 Cross patient's far arm and leg over his body.

3 Cradling his head in your hand, pull his hip sharply up and over.

4 Bend his top arm and leg at a right angle. Tilt his head back so that his chin juts forward.

In pairs

Draw up a list of 'Dos' and 'Don'ts' when giving emergency first aid to an unconscious person.

Discuss what shock is, what the symptoms are and how it should be treated.

Practise putting each other into the recovery position.

Police duties and police powers

The duties of the police force are:

1 To protect life and property.

2 To maintain public order.

3 To prevent and detect crime.

The police couldn't do anything at all without help from the general public, and most of their information comes from what people tell them. To do their job, the police obviously need to ask people questions and search their property. A lot of the law which sets out police duties and powers is contained in the Police and Criminal Evidence Act 1984.

Stopping

If a police officer stops you in the street, you are entitled to know the officer's name and the police station where he or she works. You are also entitled to know why the officer has stopped you. It is not acceptable for this to be simply because of your colour, dress, hairstyle or the fact that you might have been in trouble before.

You don't strictly have to answer an officer's questions, unless he or she suspects that you have committed (or are about to commit) an arrestable offence – such as theft, assault or carrying an offensive weapon. In these circumstances you must give your name and address, but need not answer any more questions.

REMEMBER If you're stopped by the police, keep calm and don't overreact. If you're obstructive and rude, you're more likely to be arrested. Staying calm will also help you remember what happened and what was said. Don't deliberately mislead the police by giving false information or wasting their time.

Searching

The police are allowed to search you for a number of reasons. You cannot be forced to be searched unless you have been arrested or are suspected of carrying:

■ drugs

■ stolen goods

■ weapons, or anything that might be used as a weapon

■ anything that might be used for burglary or theft.

If you are searched, the officer should explain why the search is taking place and what he or she expects to find.

Any search which involves more than a check of your outer clothing should be done out of public view or in a police station or van. If the search requires more than the removal of outer clothing, it should be done by someone of the same sex.

REMEMBER Stay calm, and make sure you know why you're being searched. If the police search you illegally, they are committing an assault, but if they have good reason, and you refuse, you may be charged with obstruction.

⣿ In groups

1 What do you learn from this page about police powers to stop and search you in the street?

2 Discuss the views on stop and search (right). Which do you agree with and why? Where appropriate, support your views by giving examples from your own experience.

" The police have too much power to interfere in our lives. The police powers of stop and search are an infringement of our liberty to move around freely. "

" If the police didn't have the powers to stop and search people it would be even easier for criminals to break the law and get away with it. "

Reprimands, Warnings and Prosecutions

Helping the police

If you are asked to go to a police station to help with enquiries it's important to know whether you are being arrested. If you are being asked to go voluntarily, you may refuse – although the police may then decide to arrest you – and then you have to go.

If you are at the police station you are entitled to send a message to your family or a friend telling them where you are, and also to free legal advice from a solicitor. If you have not been arrested, you may leave at any time you wish.

Questioning

If you are 16 or under you should never be interviewed without your parent or an appropriate adult (such as a teacher or social worker) being present. However, you should also have a solicitor present to advise you. You must give the police your name and address, but you have the right not to answer any further questions.

If you have broken the law, whether you will receive a reprimand or a warning or are prosecuted will depend on the offence, whether you admit it and how many offences you have committed.

There are now limits on how many 'last chances' the police can give you before you end up in court. If you commit a really serious offence you will be prosecuted straight away. If you commit a less serious offence, the police can give you a maximum of only two chances before you will definitely be taken to court.

As soon as you break the law, even for something you might consider minor (like dropping litter or riding a bicycle on the pavement) the police will give you a reprimand for the first time and a warning for the second time. If you break the law for a third time you will automatically be sent to court and prosecuted.

If you are given a reprimand, the police officer talks to you about what you have done and explains what will happen to you if you break the law again. They will remind you about who you have hurt by breaking the law – your family as well as your victim. The police will keep a record of your crime. You may find that your details are passed on to a Youth Offending Team who will decide if any further action should be taken.

If you are given a warning, the police will talk to you and put your crimes on record in the same way as for a reprimand. You are automatically referred to a Youth Offending Team who will generally decide what type of scheme to put you on to stop you committing any more crimes.

Reprimands and warnings can only be given to people who have admitted that they have broken the law. This means that someone who has committed an offence and does not admit it cannot be given a reprimand or warning. In these cases they will be sent to court and prosecuted.

Prosecution means your case will be heard in the youth court. If the court finds you guilty, you will be sentenced. You will then have a criminal conviction.

What records are kept on young offenders?

A record of your final warning will be kept by the police and the youth offending team until you are 18 years old. If you offend again, this will help them to decide any further action. A reprimand or final warning is not a conviction and does not constitute a criminal record.

If you are 10 or 11 years old, the records on you will stay 'live' on the Police National Computer until your 17th birthday. If you are older, the records will stay active for five years.

In groups

Discuss what you learn from this page about the system for dealing with young people who break the law. Do you think it is fair always to prosecute a person for their third offence, however minor their first two offences might have been? Give reasons for your views.

Keeping the peace

A lot of police time is spent controlling large crowds. As well as looking after crowds at football matches and other sporting events, the police also supervise demonstrations and public protest meetings. Every year the Metropolitan Police deals with several hundred demonstrations and processions in central London.

The police attend demonstrations and disputes to make sure that the law is not broken, and to protect both sides. Many demonstrations are carried out peacefully and no incidents occur. Occasionally, though, violence breaks out and the police have to act to protect people and property.

Sometimes the police are accused of causing trouble by the way they treat demonstrators. From reports you have read in the newspapers or seen on television, do you think there is any evidence that the police cause trouble at demonstrations?

❝ *The police might have been on duty at a demonstration for hours. Then you have just one flare-up as one small group gets out of hand. A few helmets roll in a scuffle, and a couple of demonstrators get dragged to a police van. It makes good television, just right for the introduction to the news bulletin, but it gives a totally false picture of what has been going on. We know for a fact that television cameras and their spotlights egg a crowd on.* ❞ – Senior police officer

In groups

Discuss times when you have been in a large crowd that the police have been controlling. Talk about the way the police handled the crowd and any incidents that occurred. What do you think of the way the police controlled the crowd?

Discuss what the senior police officer said. Do you think television often presents a distorted picture of what happens at demonstrations?

Keeping you safe

Police anti-terrorist units are at the forefront of keeping you safe from terrorist attacks.

Anti-terrorist measures include upgrading the CCTV network, following the bombings in London on July 7 2005, which showed the importance of CCTV cameras by recording the terrorists on their way from Luton to London.

The police argue that this is necessary to provide clearer images, which can be used as evidence. But some people are concerned that this is a further move towards a 'surveillance society' with cameras following your every move.

In groups

Do CCTV cameras make you feel safe or scared?

Are you worried about living in a surveillance society?

What do you think of the police?

? What do you think?

What is your attitude towards the police? On your own, study each of the statements (below) and decide whether you agree with it, disagree with it or are not sure. Then share your views in a class discussion.

1 People don't respect the police as much as they should.

2 You can rely on the police to help you if you are in trouble.

3 The police are friendly and polite.

4 The police are good at catching criminals and maintaining law and order.

5 The police are racist and treat white people better than black people and Asians.

6 The police have a difficult job to do and they do it as well as they can.

7 The police are bullies and misuse their authority.

8 Teenagers don't like the police because the police don't like teenagers.

9 The police interfere in our lives too much.

10 The media only report the mistakes the police make, not all the good things they do.

For your file

Write a short statement saying what you think of the way the police behave and what your attitude to the police is.

Doing a good job?

It is easy to see the police as a nuisance, or even as the enemy, but they are just doing a job which can save lives and try to make our society a better place.

Police regulation

Contrary to popular belief, the police are not above the law. They follow the law, just like us, and are also regulated by a separate set of guidelines. These are outlined in the Police and Criminal Evidence Act 1984 and you can get hold of a copy at your local library or police station.

An officer has broken the disciplinary code that the police must follow if he or she:

- neglects his or her duty;
- makes a false statement, written or spoken;
- misuses his or her authority;
- is abusive to a member of the public;
- is racially discriminant in any way.

You can make an official complaint if you think an officer has broken this code. Before you do, get legal advice from a solicitor – you can see one free of charge at your local Citizens Advice Bureau.

Making friends

In pairs

Discuss the list of statements about friends and friendships. Decide whether you think each statement is **a)** true, **b)** sometimes true, **c)** not true. Make a note of your views, then join up with another pair and share your views in a group discussion.

The secret of making friends

Anita Naik offers advice on how to make and keep friends

Be patient and sensitive

No matter how much you like someone, don't demand too much, too soon; it may freak the other person out. No one likes to be pushed into things, nor to feel suffocated by another's attentions. Chill out, and let the relationship grow naturally.

Listen to your own conscience

If a prospective friend does something that makes you feel uncomfortable, don't be afraid to break off. Likewise, if someone makes you feel bad about yourself, then dump them – they're no good for you. So that bad feelings aren't left to ferment and therefore cloud whatever remains of the friendship, be up front and let them know what's bugging you.

Learn to be trusting

It's impossible to have a friendship if there is no element of trust. Both people have to be open, honest and not afraid to say no.

Be forgiving

Some people just can't cut it in the friendship stakes; they may let you down, stand you up, or blab something that was meant to be just between the two of you. What you've got to do is understand the limits of particular friendships.

You must not think that one disappointing friendship means that they'll all be disappointing. Learn to understand and forgive your friends their shortcomings. There will be some people who will always be there for you, and there will be others who won't.

It's okay to have lots of friends

Without being at all disloyal, you can have different friends for different things. Some mates are ice-skating buddies, others are school pals and others you see only once a week at dance class. To some friends you will be an open book and they will know all your deepest, darkest fears. Other friends will only know the barest details. That's fine. Don't get worked up about making every friend a best friend.

What is a friend?

1. A friend must share your interests.
2. A friend is someone you can trust.
3. A friend should have a similar personality to you.
4. A friend should share your values.
5. A friend should always cover up for you.
6. A friend is someone who you can tell your private thoughts and feelings.
7. A friend is someone who won't tease you.
8. A friend must be approved of by your parents.
9. A friend is someone who won't disagree with you.
10. A friend is someone who will forgive you.

In groups

Do you agree with what Anita Naik says about how to make and keep friends?

Make lists of **a)** the kinds of behaviour that help to cement a friendship, **b)** the kinds of behaviour that are likely to destroy a friendship.

For your file

Write your views on friends and friendships. Say how important friendships are to you, what you value most in a friendship and what your expectations of friendships are.

friends and friendships

Problems with friendships

Growing ← → Apart

Quite frankly, I now find her boring a lot of the time I'm with her. But when she doesn't come round like she used to, then I miss her.'

Gemma

Most friendships start because the two people involved have lots in common, so when one of you grows up faster than the other and finds new interests it can change everything between you. If that happens, it's sad, but often the only thing to do is to have a bit of a break from being best friends and each see other friends who share your interests.

If you and your friends are growing apart …

Don't ✗ Do ✓

 make the situation into a big row so you end up falling out forever and making yourself even more unhappy. OK, so you don't have much in common with each other just now — but maybe in a few months you'll find one or both of you has changed and you might just want to be mates again! Give each other a bit of space, but try to keep in touch.

 blame yourself. This hasn't happened because you're a terrible friend or there's something wrong with you — it's simply that people change.

 feel bad if you're the one who feels you're growing out of your old mates. It's not like you're doing it on purpose and it happens to lots of people — it's all part of growing up.

 see this as an opportunity to make new mates rather than fretting too much about the past. If you're the one who's feeling dumped it's easy to wallow in self-pity and lose your confidence, but look at it this way — now you're free to find mates who you really have things in common with.

 remember that you won't be the only one going through this. It's easy to imagine everyone else is paired off already and won't want you, but if you look closer you'll probably see other mates are going through sticky patches over exactly the same kind of problem.

 confide in someone at home about what's going on so you can get a bit of extra support while you're making some new friends.

The Rules of Friendship

1 Keep secrets.
2 Wait for your friend to offer secrets; do not pry.
3 Share your happy times as well as your sad times.
4 Stand up for your friends.
5 Show loving support.
6 Ask your friends for support when you need help.
7 Offer help; do not just wait for your friend to ask.
8 Make sure you return borrowed things.
9 If your friend hurts your feelings, say so. Don't go off in a sulk.
10 Look in your friend's eyes when you talk.
11 Don't joke about or tease your friend.
12 Don't be jealous of your friend's other relationships.

⚏ In groups

Study 'The rules of friendship'. Discuss whether you agree or disagree with each one. Are there any other rules you would add to the list? Which three rules do you think are the most important?

Study the article (left). Discuss the advice that it gives on how to deal with the situation if a friend is growing apart from you.

How much are you influenced by your friends?

How do you behave when you're with your friends? Do you let your friends influence your decisions, or do you always make up your own mind and do what you think is right? Do this quiz to find out how much you let your friends influence you. Keep a record of your answers, and then check what your answers tell you about your behaviour when you are with your friends.

 1 You are with a friend and they say something you do not agree with. *Do you…*

a agree with them to avoid an argument;

b only say what you think if they ask your opinion;

c tell them you don't agree with them and explain why?

 2 Some friends dare you to do something reckless that could have serious consequences. *Do you…*

a agree to do it in order to try to impress them;

b find an excuse for not doing it;

c refuse and say you're not prepared to be so reckless?

 3 A group of your friends are teasing someone and making hurtful remarks about them. *Do you…*

a join in because they expect you to do so;

b not join in, but do nothing to stop them;

c try to get them to stop?

 4 You have become friends with someone none of the rest of your friends like. *Do you…*

a drop your new friend;

b ask your friends why they don't like your new friend then decide what to do;

c tell them that it's none of their business and you'll be friends with who you choose?

5 Your friends ask you to do something that may get you into trouble with the police. *Do you…*

a join in because everyone else is;

b try and persuade them it's wrong, but go along with them if they won't listen;

c tell them you're not joining in and walk away?

 6 Two of your friends have a row and fall out. *Do you…*

a take the side of the person you like best;

b leave them to sort it out and try not to get involved;

c listen to both sides and support whoever you think is in the right?

 7 One of your friends asks you to tell a lie to stop them getting into trouble with their parents. *Do you…*

a agree to do so because you are afraid of losing their friendship;

b say you'll only do so if you are not covering up anything serious;

c say no and explain that you can't get involved in what's going on between them and their parents?

 8 Your friends are talking about sex in a way that you don't like. *Do you…*

a join in, even though you feel uncomfortable;

b keep quiet, but not show your disapproval;

c tell them why you don't like the way they are talking?

What your answers tell you about how much you are influenced by your friends

Mostly 'a's You are so concerned about what your friends think of you that you will do almost anything to keep in with them. You're allowing them to influence you so much that you've stopped thinking for yourself. You need to listen far more to what your instincts and conscience tell you about how to behave than to think about what will most impress your friends. You must start asserting yourself and acting according to your beliefs rather than just doing things to please others.

Mostly 'b's You hesitate before saying or doing things that you don't believe in, and sometimes you allow yourself to do things that you don't want to do in order not to upset your friends. When faced with an awkward situation you tend to look for the easy way out. You need to start trusting your own judgement more and to be more prepared to speak out and do things that might set you apart from the crowd.

Mostly 'c's You have a healthy disregard for what others might think of you and are prepared to stand up for yourself and do what you believe is right. Sometimes it will cause difficulties with friends, but you understand that it is more important to stick to your principles rather than to do things just to curry favour. Your actions give you self-respect because you don't allow people to pressurise you, and those people who are your friends know where they stand with you and can rely on you to speak your mind.

In pairs

Talk about what you have learned from this activity about how much influence you let your friends have on you.

Gangs

❝ *I used to be part of a gang. But they made me do things I didn't want to do and I got into trouble. Now I steer clear of them.* ❞

❝ *Belonging to a gang is great. You really feel you're somebody. We do all kinds of crazy things together. It's a great laugh.* ❞

❝ *I think people who go round in gangs are weak. They give each other courage to do things they're too cowardly to do on their own.* ❞

Gangs – Know the Facts

☠ A gang is not simply a group of friends who hang around together. Gangs intimidate people.

☠ Gangs rule by fear, and this doesn't just apply to the people they pick on. Often, gang members get involved in trouble because they're too afraid to back out, in case they look soft. Peer pressure is very common in gangs.

☠ Although you may not be doing anything illegal, if you're part of a gang, you're more likely to attract the attention of the police. Young people's characters are often judged by who they mix with; if you hang around with a wild lot, outsiders will assume you're the same.

☠ If you are being picked on by a gang, tell your parents, teacher or any other adult in authority. It's difficult to stand up to bullies when they are part of a group and you're on your own – that's why you need adult help. Don't be afraid to ask for it.

For your file

Write a story about someone who allows a friend to pressurise them into doing something which they later regret.

In groups

Study the article 'Gangs – Know the Facts' (left). Why do people go round in gangs? Discuss the way people behave in gangs. Talk about your experiences of gangs and say what you think of the way gangs treat their members and people who aren't members.

The influence of advertising

Everywhere you go there are advertisements. Advertisers know that the more visible their product is, the more likely you are to buy it. So they are willing to spend large sums of money to promote their goods or services. An advert which interrupts the programme you are watching at peak time on TV may last for less than a minute, but the advertiser is willing to pay the TV company hundreds of thousands of pounds to broadcast it.

The money which advertisers pay to media institutions, such as TV companies, newspapers and magazines, provides them with most of their revenue. Without the money from advertising, the programmes broadcast by independent radio stations and commercial TV companies would not get made, and most of the magazines and newspapers you read would not get published.

Is advertising good or bad?

Some people would argue that it is wrong to use advertising to persuade people to buy things, especially things they might not really need. They also think that many advertisements are not strictly truthful when they claim that this washing powder is new and improved, or that cats love this particular brand of cat food.

The other side of the argument is that without advertising people would be less aware of what was available for them to buy. Also, that if manufacturers compete with one another to produce goods then they must compete to sell them as well.

How much influence do adverts have on you?

Some people argue that adverts have less influence than is often made out. They say that most people are suspicious of the claims that advertisers make. They suggest that the most popular TV ads are enjoyed because they are entertaining and funny, rather than because they are informative about the product, and that they don't really influence people to buy the product.

However, there is plenty of evidence to suggest that advertising does work. Retailers are often informed before a TV advertising campaign is about to take place in their area, so that they can stock up on the product in advance, and be in a position to meet the demand for the product that a campaign is likely to generate. Successful campaigns do lead to increased sales.

In groups

How much do you think you are influenced by advertisements? Talk about your favourite TV ads and why you like them. Are they for products that you are likely to go out and buy? If so, do you think the adverts have made you more likely to go out and buy them?

Discuss the views below. Say why you think advertising is either a good thing or a bad thing.

❝ *Advertising encourages people to be materialistic and to want things they don't really need.* ❞

❝ *There's nothing wrong with advertising. It keeps people informed and encourages competition which benefits everybody.* ❞

Advertising and children

Rule 1 Misleadingness

Advertisements addressed to young listeners must not exaggerate or mislead about the size, qualities or capabilities of products.

Rule 2 Prices

Prices of products advertised to younger listeners must not be minimised by words such as 'only' or 'just'.

Rule 3 Immaturity and Credulity

Advertisements must not take advantage of the immaturity or natural credulity of children.

Rule 4 Inferiority

Advertisements must not lead children to believe that unless they have or use the product they will be inferior in some way to other children or liable to be held in contempt or ridicule.

Rule 5 Direct Exhortation

Advertisements must neither encourage children to pester nor directly urge children to buy products or to ask adults to buy products for them. For example, children must not be directly invited to 'ask Mum' or 'ask Dad' to buy them an advertiser's product.

Rule 6 Appeals to Loyalty

Advertisements must not take advantage of the sense of loyalty of children or suggest that, unless children buy or encourage others to buy a product or service, they will be failing in some duty or lacking in loyalty.

Rule 7 Distance Selling to Children

Advertisements must not invite children to purchase products by mail or telephone, including fax, email and via the internet.

Rule 8 Competitions

a) References to competitions for children are acceptable provided that any skill required is appropriate to the age of likely participants, and the value of the prizes and the chance of winning are not exaggerated.

b) The published rules must be submitted in advance to the licensee and the principal conditions of the competition must be included in the advertisement.

Rule 9 Free Gifts

References to 'free' gifts for children in advertisements must include all qualifying conditions, e.g. any time limit, how many products need to be bought, how many wrappers need to be collected, etc.

Rule 10 Health and Hygiene

a) Advertising must not condone inappropriate health standards for children.

b) Advertising must not suggest that confectionery and snack food products may be substituted for balanced meals.

Rule 11 Child Voiceovers and Presentation

a) Children may take part in radio commercials, subject to all relevant legal requirements. However, they must not feature in advertisements in ways which might cause them moral harm, give concern about their welfare or be regarded as commercial exploitation.

b) Children used in commercials must not be used to present selling messages and calls to action about products or services which are likely to be beyond their understanding or which the law prevents them from buying themselves.

Rule 12 Testimonials

Children must not personally testify about products and services. They may, however, give spontaneous comments on matters in which they would have an obvious natural interest.

Rule 13 Food and Soft Drinks Advertisements

Advertisers must follow strict guidelines concerning nutrition and health claims for foods. Promotional offers to children must be used with a due sense of responsibility. Similarly, licensed characters and celebrities popular with children must be used with a due sense of responsibility.

The Advertising Standards Authority regulates the content of advertisements and has codes for TV, radio and all other forms of advertising. The codes contain special rules for advertisers who target children aged 15 and below. The advertisements must not include any material which might result in harm to them either physically, mentally or morally. The detailed rules which radio advertisers must observe when they target young people are shown above.

 In groups

Study carefully the guidelines for advertising and children and discuss the reasons for each part of the code.

In Sweden, television advertisements aimed at children under twelve are banned, because it is argued that young children cannot tell the difference between television advertising and other programmes until they are ten. Sweden would like to see TV adverts aimed at children banned in all EU countries. Do you think such a ban should be introduced in the UK? Give reasons for your views.

Getting the message across

The Commercial Break

Television advertisers use various techniques to get their message across on television. They mix people and places, words and music with pictures and they choose very carefully what and who they show in their advertisements. The timing of television commercials is very important as well. Advertisers know, from market research, exactly when most mothers, children or families are likely to be viewing. They plan their advertising campaigns accordingly.

People and Places

The people you see in television advertisements are often not like real people. Sometimes they represent a kind of person – a stereotype – and we understand the message the stereotype conveys. For example: if we see a man in a suit carrying a briefcase we recognize a businessman and understand the message is about efficiency; if we see a woman with a baby, feeding or playing with it, we understand the message is about caring. These messages are very important in advertising.

The people in television advertisements are usually attractive, young, quite well-off and white. There are sometimes old people and children, but only if the product is something especially for them. People who are poor, unattractive or physically disabled are hardly ever seen in advertisements.

Sometimes famous people, sports personalities or television stars are paid to advertise products. The advertiser thinks that if you like the person you will believe what they say and trust them. Or you might secretly admire them and want to be like them, so you would like to use the product they advertise.

Words and Music

The words of advertisements are obviously very important. Short, snappy, easy-to-remember slogans are often the key to success in an advertising campaign.

Jingles are those catchy little rhymes and verses which are easy to pick up, sing along with or remember after only one or two hearings.

It is also fashionable now for advertisers to use 'real' music in their advertisements so that the song and the product become closely linked together. If you liked the song that will encourage you to buy the product.

⠿ In groups

Discuss what you learn from the article 'The Commercial Break' and draw up a list of the various techniques that are used in TV advertisements. Talk about recent TV ads and discuss which of these techniques they use.

Imagine you were in charge of planning a TV advertising campaign for a new product aimed at young people of your age, for example, a new bicycle model. Discuss your ideas for a 30 second advert and prepare a proposal to present to the rest of the class.

Plan and produce a radio advert for a new product. Discuss how many radio adverts include a catchy piece of music with simple lyrics called a jingle. Draft your script, choose appropriate music and compose a jingle to advertise your product. Then make a tape recording of your advert and play it to the rest of the class.

For your file

Find an advert in a newspaper or magazine and write an analysis of it. Comment on what its message is, who it is aimed at and how the words and picture(s) are used to create an image of the product that will encourage the target audience to want to buy it.

Sponsorship

Another way companies use the power of the media to get their message across is through **sponsorship**. One form of sponsorship involves paying for the right to have their name associated with a particular event. An example of this is when a company sponsors a sporting event so that the advertiser's name forms part of the event's title. In the 2008-9 season English football teams played each other in the Barclays Premier League and the Coca Cola Championship and teams from the lower divisions competed in the Blue Square Leagues. Every time the event is reported in the press, on the radio or TV, the sponsor gets a mention.

Another form of sponsorship involves paying teams or individuals to wear names and logos printed on their clothes. Sporting celebrities sponsored by sportswear companies include footballers David Beckham sponsored by Adidas, Wayne Rooney sponsored by Nike and John Terry sponsored by Umbro.

Celebrityendorsement

Advertisers use celebrities to promote their products because it helps them to make their brands stand out. Using a celebrity helps what is known as the recognition factor.

It also increases the chances of getting press coverage. Every time their celebrity gets their face in a newspaper or magazine it increases the possibility of their being associated with the product they are endorsing.

 In groups

Would you buy something just because a famous person plugged it? According to Bryony Gordon, it depends on the star and the product. Discuss this view.

Study this list of celebrities: Myleene Klass, David Beckham, Carol Vordeman, Lewis Hamilton, Michael Winner, Jamie Oliver, Keira Knightley, Kate Moss, Chris Moyles, Sharon Osbourne, Victoria Beckham, Coleen McLoughlin. Discuss which ones are most likely to influence you to buy the product or service that they are endorsing? Which are the least likely?

Are you making the most of your leisure time?

A test-yourself quiz

Do this quiz to find out about how well you spend your leisure time. Keep a record of your answers, and then check what your answers tell you about what use you make of your leisure time.

1 At the weekend do you:
a always plan in advance what you are going to do;
b sometimes plan things in advance;
c never plan ahead – just wait to see what happens?

2 How much time do you spend each week on your hobby?
a 4–6 hours;
b 1–3 hours;
c less than an hour a week.

3 What types of TV programmes do you mainly watch?
a 'serious' programmes, such as documentaries, news and drama;
b a mixture of serious programmes and light entertainment;
c light entertainment, such as comedies, soaps, pop music and quizzes.

4 How often do you stay after school for a club or a practice?
a 2 or 3 times a week;
b once a week;
c hardly ever.

5 When you go out with your friends do you usually:
a go somewhere to do something, for example, go to a film or a disco, or to a park to play football;
b go shopping or to a café;
c hang about hoping someone might suggest something to do?

6 How often do you read a book other than a schoolbook?
a most days;
b every now and then;
c hardly ever.

7 How often do you take exercise (apart from in PE lessons)?
a 5–6 days a week;
b 2–3 days a week;
c hardly ever.

8 When you go on a computer what do you mostly use it for?
a finding information from the Internet;
b visiting social networking sites;
c playing games.

9 How do you keep up with what's going on in the world?
a by watching the news/reading a newspaper daily;
b by watching the news every now and then;
c by relying on other people to tell you if something happens.

making the most of your leisure

10 If you are asked to volunteer to take part in a community activity do you usually:

a volunteer;

b wait to see if your friends do, then volunteer;

c never volunteer?

11 How often in the holidays do you feel bored because you can't think of anything to do?

a very rarely;

b sometimes;

c most days.

12 How much time each day do you spend watching TV?

a less than 1 hour;

b between 1 and 3 hours;

c over 3 hours.

What your answers say about how you spend your leisure time

Mostly 'a's You make very good use of your leisure time. You have plenty of interests and hobbies and you plan activities to do at the weekend and with your friends. You are prepared to volunteer for things and are involved in after-school activities. You look after yourself too by taking plenty of exercise. So you shouldn't get bored. But make sure you don't wear yourself out with all your activities. Allow yourself some time just to relax!

Mostly 'b's Your attitude to your leisure time is the same as many people's. Sometimes you plan ahead and you get actively involved in the things you like doing on a fairly regular basis. You've got a more relaxed attitude to life than the people who get mostly 'a's. But you could be making better use of your leisure time than you are. If you want to achieve more in your leisure pursuits, you'll need to put your mind to doing so.

Mostly 'c's You're not getting as much out of your leisure time as you could be. If your life seems boring much of the time, then you need to ask yourself why. Things won't change unless you do something to make them. Otherwise you'll continue to drift through life getting less out of it than you could be.

Four Ways to Make Better Use of Your Leisure Time

1 Ration how much TV you watch.

2 Stay at school once a week for an after-school club.

3 Go out for a jog or a bike ride every other day.

4 Spend at least 20 minutes a day reading a book, magazine or newspaper.

In pairs

Talk about what you have learned from this activity. How well do you use your leisure time and how good are you at:

- planning how you spend your time;
- getting involved in activities at school and in the community;
- using your leisure time to develop your knowledge and skills?

Each decide on one or more things you could do to make better use of your leisure time.

I never have any time to myself

" My problem is I hardly get any time to myself. By the time I've done my chores and then my homework, I'm exhausted. All I want to do is watch TV or listen to my DVDs. And at the weekend I never have any time to myself because I'm expected to do things with the family. What can I do? It's really getting me down. " – Peta

For your file

Read Peta's letter (left). Write a reply to Peta advising her on how to deal with her problem.

Beating the boredom blues

So it's the school holidays. For once you've got time on your hands. The trouble is: you don't seem to know what to do with it. Samantha Graham suggests ten things you can do to beat those school holiday boredom blues.

Getting a Piece of the Action

1 Join The Club

Many youth clubs run schemes for teenagers during the holidays, or there may be one being run at your school. Go and find out what's on offer by asking at your local community centre or looking in the community newsletter.

2 Go Exploring

Investigate the area where you live. Many people never bother to visit the interesting places in their neighbourhood. Find out about places you can visit and things to see in your area from the local tourist information office or from your local library.

3 Get Into Shape

Oh no! I hear you groan, but getting fit can be fun. One of the best forms of exercise is swimming, another is cycling. You don't need to have a 21-gear racer or a mountain bike. You can go at your own speed and explore all those places that you've never got round to seeing.

4 Go Green

Contact organisations like Friends of the Earth and see if there are any local schemes to protect the environment that you can get involved in. Or organise your own scheme. For example, get together with some friends and set up a recycling team.

5 Do-It-Yourself

Do a deal with your parents. Say that if they let you redesign and redecorate your bedroom and supply you with the materials, you'll do the work yourself. You'll not only learn all about painting and decorating, but you'll also end up with the bedroom you've always wanted.

6 Put It In Writing

Get your pen and paper out and get writing. So you never got round to keeping a diary? Well, now's the time to start! Or what about that story that's been lurking at the back of your mind, or that letter you said you'd write to the newspaper in protest about cruelty to animals? Get scribbling.

7 Get Crafty

Ask your mum or dad if you can borrow their tools and get out into the shed and make something for yourself. What about a new DVD rack? Raid your money box to buy some of that material you fancied and make yourself something new to wear. Use your practical skills – get crafty!

8 Get In On The Act

Join the local drama club and get involved in their productions. You don't fancy acting? Then get a back-stage role, looking after the lighting, painting the scenery, making the costumes or doing the make-up. Or get together with your friends, borrow a video camera and make your own video.

9 Read All About It

Get down to the local library and borrow those expensive books about your hobby that you couldn't afford to buy. Become more of an expert than you already are on the things that really interest you.

10 Get Connected

Everyone's been telling you to develop your computer skills. Well, now's your chance. Get on-line and search the net for websites about your favourite subject. Find an e-mail buddy who's into your hobby and swap information and advice. You could even design your own newsletter to send to your family and friends.

In groups

Discuss Samantha Graham's suggestions. Talk about the ones which appeal to you most and the ones which appeal to you least. Can you suggest other ways of beating boredom and making the most of your leisure time? Keep notes of your ideas and share them in a class discussion.

Choose your exercise

One way you can use your leisure time well is to make sure you get enough exercise. The fitter you are, the more energy you will have. The more energy you have, the more you will be able to get out of life.

True physical fitness is something more than simply being fit to cope with the stresses and strains of everyday life. It consists of three important ingredients – stamina, suppleness and strength – the S-factors (see box).

First and most important is **STAMINA**. This is staying power, endurance, the ability to keep going without gasping for breath. For stamina, you need a well-developed circulation in the heart and lungs so that plenty of vital oxygen is pumped to your working muscles. With stamina you have a slower, more powerful heartbeat. You can cope more easily with prolonged or heavy exertion.

Next is **SUPPLENESS** or flexibility. You need to develop maximum range of movement of your neck, spine and joints to avoid spraining ligaments and pulling muscles and tendons. The more mobile you are, the less likely you'll suffer aches and pains brought on by stiffness.

Finally, **STRENGTH**. Extra muscle-power in reserve for those often unexpected heavier jobs. Lifting and shifting need strong shoulder, trunk and thigh muscles. Toned-up tummy muscles help to take the strain … and keep your waistline trim.

For your file

❝ Why do adults make such a fuss about teenagers taking exercise? I can't see the point myself. As far as I'm concerned exercise is a waste of time. ❞ **– Sam**

Write a reply to Sam explaining why exercise is important and suggesting the different ways she or he could get some exercise.

S-FACTOR SCORE

	Stamina	Suppleness	Strength
Canoeing	***	**	***
Climbing Stairs	***	*	**
Cricket	*	**	*
Cycling (hard)	****	**	***
Dancing (ballroom)	*	***	*
Dancing (disco)	***	****	*
Digging (garden)	***	**	****
Football	***	***	***
Gymnastics	**	****	***
Housework (moderate)	*	**	*
Jogging	****	**	**
Judo	**	****	**
Rowing	****	**	****
Swimming (hard)	****	****	****
Tennis	**	***	**
Walking (briskly)	**	*	*
Weightlifting	*	*	****
Yoga	*	****	*

* No real effect   *** Very good effect
** Beneficial effect   **** Excellent effect

In pairs

Talk about the S-factors, discussing why each one is important.

Study the S-factor score chart. Work out a test-yourself quiz, consisting of statements some of which are true and some of which are false, then give the quiz to another group to do. Here is one possible question:

1. Housework builds up your stamina more than digging. True or false?

How employment and unemployment affect the local community

When the economy is doing well, and there is full employment, people will have money to spend. They will spend their money on lots of different things, such as buying food, servicing the car or decorating the house. This creates employment for the people who do these jobs. These people in turn earn money, which they can spend elsewhere.

But this cycle can also work in reverse. If people lose their jobs, they will spend less money in the area. A factory closing can be disastrous for a local community, as many people lose their jobs at the same time. Suddenly, there is a lot less money being spent in the local community. This can mean the local garage or café goes out of business.

Because of this, the government tries to help people stay in work. When a factory closes, it provides help and support for people to find new jobs and stay in the area. Often they have to learn different skills before they can start a new job. This is known as retraining. They may have to attend a course run by a business or a local college.

Key terms

A person is **employed** when they have a job that they are paid for doing.

If someone is **unemployed** it means that a person doesn't have a job and they are looking for work.

The **workforce** means people between 18 and 65 who can work.

The Government aims to have 95% of the workforce at work. This is known as **full employment**. Because there are always some people moving from one job to another, it is impossible to have everyone working at once.

Strong economy – full employment → People spend money on goods and services → This creates employment for other people → Those people spend money in the economy

Different types of employment

Primary industry

Industry is divided into three main areas. Primary industry involves the production of raw materials through either agriculture, mining or fishing. Farmer, miner and fisherman are all examples of jobs in primary industry. In the past, many people were involved working in this sector of the economy. Today, there are very few, and numbers are declining.

'My name's Frank. I work as a fisherman, based in the port of Grimsby in the north-east of England. It's not like when I started work as a young lad. There used to be a lot more boats here. Part of the problem is over-fishing - people taking too much out of the natural environment so there are fish for today, but not tomorrow. So the EU says we have to be careful how much we fish.'

Secondary industry

This is making things out of raw materials – manufacturing. From 1850 to 1950, many people worked in manufacturing industries. Examples include the car industry, which made cars all over the UK. Since the Second World War, the number of people working in manufacturing has gone down dramatically. Many of these jobs have transferred abroad to developing countries such as China and India.

'My name's Joe. I work as a car assembly worker in Coventry – putting headlamps on cars. Things have changed here. The Jaguar factory I work at isn't British any more – it's owned by an Indian company, Tatta. And there's a lot more robots and machines in the factory. Still, it's good to be working on cars.

I know many friends who have lost their jobs, and had to retrain to do different work.'

Tertiary industry

This consists of jobs in what is known as the service sector. Here, people are providing other people with a service of some kind. Examples of service sector workers include nurses, teachers and call centre advisors. The growth in call centres, where people work together on the telephone, has been so big in recent years that now 1–2% of the entire workforce work in call centres, answering telephone calls.

'My name's Liz. I work in a call centre in Poole, dealing with enquiries for Barclays Bank. There's a whole floor of us here – over a hundred people. We all work together to deal with customers' problems. I like working in the service sector. It's good to have contact with lots of different people.'

UK employment structure

Primary industry 2%

Secondary industry 22%

Tertiary industry 76%

In groups

Study the pie chart. What does this tell you about jobs in the UK economy? Where are there fewer jobs? Where are there more jobs? Which sector of the economy can you see yourself working in? Explain why.

For your file

Explain how employment and unemployment affect the local community.
Study the Situations Vacant advertisements in your local newspaper. What does this tell you about the jobs that are available in your local area? Write a paragraph for your file explaining what this tells you about the local economy.

Employment for life

In the past, people used to talk about employment for life. The expectation was that when you finished studying you would find a job and that you would do the same job until the day you retired. This was very common for the majority of the 20th century.

Employability for life

Today, people talk about employability for life. Most people will have several different jobs during their working life. The idea is that you may either want to change jobs or be forced to change jobs, for example by being made redundant. Either way, you will still be employable. In other words, you will always be able to get a job.

Jackie's story

"I left school at 16 to become a hairdresser. But after a year's training I decided I didn't like it, and the money didn't pay well enough. So I went back to college and re-trained as a secretary. I worked as a secretary for a local building company for nine years, until I decided to start a family.

Now that my children are at school, I've decided to go back to work. I'm now working in a call centre part time for a local bank. It's good because the hours fit around school hours, so I can still look after my kids.

Eventually, I hope to progress at the call centre. That means becoming a team leader, in charge of a team of six, and eventually a call centre manager."

In groups

Compare the stories of Alfred, Jackie and Mike. Discuss how Jackie's and Mike's experiences are different from Alfred's.

For your file

Imagine you have been asked to write an article for a magazine about working lives and how they have changed in the past 60 years. Interview a number of adults, including some older people, about the jobs they have done during their lives, then draft your article.

Alfred's story

"I only had one job. At 14, my dad told me it was time to leave school and go down the pit. That was the coal pit. It was the job that most people got in our village. You either went down the pit, or you left for another job.

I worked as a miner all my working life. That's how it was during the last century till the demand for coal dropped and they started closing down most of the mines.

Even my brother Bill who left the village and went to work in a glass factory did the same job all his life. It was what you expected.

It's not the same nowadays. I look at my grand children and marvel at all the different jobs they have had. Life has certainly changed a lot over the last 50 years."

Mike's story

"I'm only 22 and I've already have five jobs. I did some temping when I was 16 in a local wood yard and a plastics factory. By the time I was 18 I was working in a bar part time, to help me through college. One summer I did Camp America — working with American school kids providing adventure activities in the holidays.

I've just graduated with a degree in business studies and I'm working in a sales job for a large company. But I don't expect to be doing this for ever. One day I hope to be running my own business."

Transferable skills

While many jobs require some skills that are specific to that particular job, many of the skills you need are the same. Since they can be transferred from one job to another, they are known as transferable skills.

Surveys of employers show that they are looking for people who:

- can communicate effectively with colleagues and customers
- have good interpersonal skills and can work in teams
- are good at solving problems
- are numerate and have experience of handling money
- have good ICT skills
- are willing and able to learn
- are flexible in their approach to work.

These skills are transferable between many jobs, so it is important that you develop them while you are at school or college. The more you have developed these skills, the more employable you will be throughout your working life.

In groups

1 Look at the list of jobs. Talk about the skills they require. If you were interviewing people for these jobs, decide which would be the three main transferable skills you would look for in candidates for each job. (Refer back to the list above.)

2 Think about any jobs you have done (for example, a paper round or some voluntary work). What transferable skills did you learn from each job? Which skills would you like to improve in the future?

* sales assistant
* hotel receptionist
* chef
* car mechanic
* bank clerk
* care assistant
* laboratory technician
* call centre worker
* plumber

For your file

How good are you at the transferable skills listed above? Rate yourself for each skill on a five point scale: 5 excellent, 4 very good, 3 good, 2 not very good, 1 poor.
Write a short statement explaining which skills you need to work hard at developing. Say why it is important for you to develop those skills.

Alcohol – the facts

What's all the fuss about?

Alcohol is certainly part of everyday life in our society. But alcohol is a powerful and potentially addictive drug, and you need to be aware of its effects.

In the short term

When you drink, the alcohol is absorbed into your bloodstream. It takes about five to ten minutes to take effect, but the effects can last for several hours. Of course, how alcohol affects you depends on how much you have drunk, how quickly you've drunk it, how strong it is and whether you've had anything to eat beforehand.

And the effects? Alcohol can make you feel great – relaxed, confident etc. It can also make you feel terrible: sick, dizzy, headachy, clumsy. It's a bit of a myth that alcohol cheers people up – it is actually a depressant and you may end up crying into your drink rather than having a laugh.

Because alcohol reduces self control, there's a real danger of people hurting themselves or others. There's the risk of drinking too much, falling asleep and choking on their own vomit. Then there's the hangover – waking up and knowing that if you move your head will split open, but you have to get up and go to school or work.

In the long term

If you're healthy anyway, and if you drink in moderation (i.e. at most a couple of drinks a day), you shouldn't have a long-term problem with alcohol. But if you drink heavily over a long period you run the risk of brain damage, liver disease (called cirrhosis), mouth and throat cancer, heart problems and stomach ulcers.

People often forget that alcohol is full of calories, hence the 'beer gut' of heavy beer drinkers. One pint of beer contains about 180 calories.

Alcohol can be addictive and you can become dependent on it. Several hundred thousand people in Britain are thought to be alcoholics. Some of them are not much older than you.

Never mix alcohol with other drugs – it can be fatal.

Drink strengths

People often think that certain drinks, such as beer or cider, contain less alcohol than others. In fact, a half a pint of ordinary strength beer or cider has about the same amount of alcohol in it as a normal glass of wine or a pub measure of whisky.

1 unit =

| half a pint of ordinary beer or cider | a single measure of spirits (whisky, gin, bacardi, vodka, etc.) | a very small glass of wine | a third of a can of strong lager |

The alcohol content of drinks is measured in units. The safe limits for adults are considered to be 14 units a week for women and 21 units a week for men. Depending on your age and your size, your safe limits may be much lower.

On average it takes an hour for the alcohol to register in the body, and then one hour per unit of alcohol drunk for it to disappear

Did you know?

It is dangerous to drink when you are pregnant. Heavy drinking can affect the baby's health and weight at birth.

 In groups

❝ *People who don't drink are party-poopers. They just don't know how to have a good time. Why should we take any notice of what they say? The risks of drinking are exaggerated.* ❞ **Kirstie (15)**

❝ *I think the people of my age who drink are immature. They do it to show off and try to make themselves popular. But they don't impress me when they start throwing up.* ❞ **Shareen (14)**

Discuss the views of these young people and say why you agree or disagree with them.

drinking and alcohol

Teenage drinking

Alcohol and Young People – the Law

Buying alcohol You are not allowed to buy alcohol until you are 18. A shopkeeper or pub landlord can be prosecuted for selling alcohol to anyone under 18. If you are under 18 and try to buy or drink alcohol on licensed premises you can be fined. Anyone who buys you a drink in a bar when you are under 18 is committing an offence. But over 16 year olds can be bought some drinks in a restaurant to have with a meal – beer and cider in England and Wales; beer, cider and wine in Scotland.

Drinking alcohol When you are 14 you are allowed to go into a licensed bar, but it is an offence for you to drink alcohol in a licensed bar if you are under 18. The police can confiscate alcohol from anyone under 18 who is drinking it in a public place. However, it is not illegal for under 18s to drink alcohol either at home or at someone else's home.

Shock Tactics In Binge Drinking Ads

Adapted from Sky News 18 June 2008

'You wouldn't start a night like this, so why end it that way?' is the message, designed to show the consequences of drinking too much.

One TV ad depicts a young man getting ready for a night out who rips out his ear-ring, smashes a wardrobe door in his face, urinates on his shoes and pours a takeaway down his shirt.

Another shows a pretty young woman arranging vomit in her hair, smudging make-up down her face and ripping her clothes.

The campaign challenges people to think twice about the consequences of losing control.

Binge-drinking not only damages your health but makes you vulnerable to harm.

If you get drunk you are much more likely to be involved in an accident or assault, be charged with a criminal offence, contract a sexually transmitted infection or have an unplanned pregnancy.

 In groups

What do the articles suggest are the risks a person runs if they get very drunk? What do you think of people who get very drunk? How would you describe their behaviour – funny? stupid? disgusting? immature?

What is your opinion of someone who deliberately tries to get someone drunk?

In pairs

Study the information on these two pages and produce a True or False quiz, consisting of statements about alcohol and drinking. Then give the quiz to another pair to do.

For your file

Design a poster called 'Think Before You Drink' to make young people of your age aware of how drinking can affect them.

Problem drinking

Kerry'sStory

Kerry, 14, started drinking for a laugh with her mates. But now she's relying on it more and more ...

'If you'd said to me a while ago that I'd be drinking most weekends when I reached this age, I'd never have believed you. When I was younger and my mum and dad let me try their drinks, I always thought they were disgusting – I couldn't see why anyone would want to drink them because they tasted so horrible.

Confidence

That all changed when my mate Ailsa got her brother to buy us some cider one night. We were supposed to be seeing some lads in the park later on and we had it before we met them. Ailsa said it tasted okay and would give us confidence and she was right – I couldn't believe how good it made me feel. I've always been quite a shy and nervous person, but after a few swigs of cider, I felt really good. Ailsa and I were laughing at everything and I became much more loud and confident. I felt really good about myself – much better than I normally did.

'That night we met the lads in the park. Normally, I'd have been so quiet and shy with them, but because I'd had some cider I felt great and I actually got off with James, the boy I'd fancied for ages.

Cider

'After that Ailsa and I would split a bottle of cider between us whenever we were going somewhere, like to a mate's party. Then I started feeling like I needed a drink to get me in the mood for enjoying myself, even if we were just going down the park to hang around. If I haven't had a drink and there are lads there I feel all panicky and shaky and don't usually say much to them.

'I spend a fortune on breath fresheners because my mum would kill me if she ever found out that I'm drinking, and all my pocket money seems to go on cider these days. I know I'm probably relying on drink too much now but at least I'm having fun.'

Valerie's Story

'My father died when I was nine and I think it was then that my mother started drinking heavily. It was a horrific situation because I felt so helpless. I would come home and she'd be sitting in front of the TV completely drunk. Very often there would be no food on the table and no money to buy any because she'd spent it all on drink. Sometimes I'd have to go round to a friend's house and beg them to lend us some money – it was so humiliating.'

Gradually her mother's problem became more serious and it was Valerie who had to run the home. 'I had two younger brothers to look after as well, which was no joke. I used to come home with heaps of homework only to spend my evenings cooking, cleaning and doing the laundry. It was very difficult because I really wanted to go to university but I couldn't fit in time for studying.'

For Valerie, the worst thing was the uncertainty. 'I'd never know quite what to expect when I came home.

One day I'd come in and she'd be rolling around on the kitchen floor, so drunk that she'd wet herself. I would have to clean her up and put her to bed like a baby.'

Valerie tried everything she could. She joined a local branch of Alateen. She tried to get her mother to join a support group to kick the habit. But although her mother tried to change, the attempts were usually short-lived. 'I felt very guilty about it. I began to think that maybe I was to blame for her drinking, and that I had to make her stop. I also felt guilty about wanting to leave and go to college when I knew that there would be no one to look after her or my younger brothers, and I realised that I had to make a difficult choice.'

In the end she got a place at a college 20 miles away so she could still live at home. Now 20 and in her second year, she is finding it more and more difficult to keep up with course work and look after the family. 'I'm a bit fed up because I am missing out on all the social life and, whenever a guy asks me out, I usually have to turn him down. I sometimes wish that someone would pay attention to me for a change – Mum has always been the centre of attention because of her problem. All I can hope is that one day she will get over this.'

⚏ In groups

Discuss Kerry's story. Do you think she has a problem or is she just having fun? What would you say to her to persuade her to cut down her drinking?

Discuss the problems that Valerie has had to face because of her mother's alcoholism. What do you learn about what it feels like to have a parent with a drinking problem?

For your file

Study the advice on how to cope. Imagine you write an advice column for a teenage magazine. Write your reply to a letter from Tony (13) who lives alone with his father. His father has a drink problem and Tony is trying to cope.

Living with Someone who Drinks – How to Cope

Look after yourself and take steps to protect yourself, especially if you think you might be at risk.

Don't blame yourself for their drinking. Each adult is responsible for him or herself.

Don't pour away alcohol unless someone asks you. Taking alcohol from someone who is already drunk may put you at risk of being hurt.

Don't cover up or make excuses to other people for their drinking.

Don't be afraid to voice your concerns when they are sober.

Tell another adult you trust what's going on. Share the burden.

Contact Alateen and Al-Anon Family Groups. They are organisations which aim to help families of problem drinkers. Alateen deal specifically with teenagers who have been, or still are, affected by an alcoholic relative. The organisation is completely confidential.

ALATEEN, 61 Great Dover Street, London SE1 4YF
Tel: 020 7403 0888
www.al-anonuk.org.uk/alateen

Change and the school community – the six term year

Your school is a community of people with a common aim – to provide you with an education that will enable you to make the fullest use of your talents and that will prepare you for life as an adult citizen.

The school community is made up of lots of different groups of people: students, teachers, classroom assistants, administrative staff, caretaking and cleaning staff, parents and governors. Whenever a major change is made – for example, to the size of the school, the hours of the school day or the number of terms in the school year – it will affect all these groups.

A new school year?

Traditionally, the pattern of the school year in England has been three terms:

- a long winter term with a week's half-term in the middle, followed by a break of about a fortnight at Christmas.

- a spring term, varying in length according to the date of Easter, with a week for half-term, followed by a break of about a fortnight over Easter.

- a summer term with the first half varying in length because of the date of Easter, with a week's half-term, followed by a long summer holiday, often of seven or eight weeks.

A government enquiry recommended in 2001 that local education authorities, which decide the pattern of the school year, should introduce a standard school year of six terms. The six-term year would consist of:

- two terms before Christmas

- no term longer than 38 days (seven weeks and three days)

- a two-week October break between terms 1 and 2

- a break of two weeks over Christmas between terms 2 and 3

- four terms after Christmas of no longer than six weeks each

- a week's break between terms 3 and 4 and terms 5 and 6 (traditional spring and summer half-term)

- the break between terms 4 and 5 being fixed each year, instead of varying according to the date of Easter

- a summer break of always more than five weeks.

However the government believes that decisions on term dates and holidays should be made locally, so while schools in some local authorities have adopted the six- term year, others still have the traditional three-term pattern.

A change for the better?

Here are some reactions to the proposal to change to a six-term year.

" How would everyone manage to fit in their holidays during a shorter summer break? It's hard enough as it is trying to get time off when everyone else wants it. "
– Parent

" It would increase the pressure on teachers, who would lose the advantage of having a long block of time in the summer in which to do detailed planning. "
– Teacher

" It might ease the frantic scramble there is at the beginning of the autumn term to sort everything out, by spreading things over the year a bit more. "
– School secretary

" You don't want to be in school in the summer when it's hot. I'd much rather have a long summer holiday than lots of short breaks throughout the year. " –
Student

" I'm all for it. Children get out of the habit of studying during the summer holiday. It's always a fight to get them to do their homework when they go back in the autumn. " – Parent

" We do a lot of maintenance work in the summer holidays at present. But we should be able to fit it in whatever the pattern of the school year. " – Caretaker

" Research shows that many children have forgotten what they have learned when they return to school after a six-week break. I think it would help us to improve the school's academic results. " – Governor

In groups

List what you think to be the advantages and disadvantages of having a six-term school year, taking into consideration how it would affect all members of the school community.

Organise a debate on the motion: 'This house believes that a six-term school year is better than a three-term school year.'

The school day

In groups

Talk about how your school day is organised. Imagine you have been asked to inquire into ways of changing it. What are the arguments for and against:

a an earlier start or a later start;

b longer or shorter morning/afternoon breaks;

c a longer lunch hour;

d an earlier or a later finishing time?

Consider other ideas, such as reorganising the lesson timetable so that all the lessons take place on four and a half days – activities could then be organised on the other half-day to allow students to pursue their own interests. In your discussions, take into consideration how your suggestions would affect the various different members of the school's community.

Decide whether or not you recommend any changes to the school day. Appoint a spokesperson to report your conclusions to the rest of the class in a class discussion.

Participating in the school community

School councils

Most schools have a school council which exists to let the teachers and headteacher know what students' opinions are on a range of school issues. The school council usually consists of two or three elected representatives from each year group.

Year councils

Because school councils are sometimes dominated by older students, some schools have introduced year councils. The aim of a year council is to give students the opportunity to express opinions on matters of importance to that particular year group.

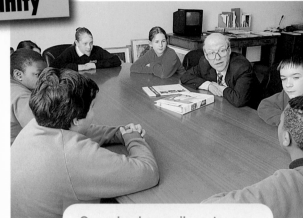

Our school council meets once every three weeks. It discusses issues such as the dress code, the use of social areas, charity fundraising and bullying.

Beach Lane School Year 8 Council – Constitution

1. The council's purpose is to act as a forum for discussion of school issues relevant to Year 8, and to let the teachers and headteacher know what student opinion is on these issues. The council will also take responsibility for co-operating with year staff in the organisation of one social event per term for Year 8.

2. Membership of the council will consist of three representatives from each class, elected on a termly basis.

3. Meetings will be held once a fortnight. The council members will elect a chair to control the meetings and a secretary who will be responsible for circulating the agenda for each meeting and taking and circulating minutes of meetings.

4. The class representatives will be responsible for giving a report of the council's meetings to their class. Agenda and minutes of meetings will be put up in each classroom.

5. The Year 8 council will elect two of its members to be members of the school council, with responsibility for raising issues on behalf of Year 8 students at school council meetings.

6. The chair, secretary and school council representatives will be responsible for taking up matters raised at council meetings with the year head and other teachers, and for reporting back on such matters to the Year 8 council.

7. The head of year will attend all council meetings as an observer and both they and the other year staff will be available as required to offer support and advice to council members and to assist in the settlement of disputes.

In groups

Imagine that elections are about to be held for class representatives to the Year 8 council. Choose one of the group to stand as a candidate. Together draft a statement of the issues you think the Year 8 council should take up for your candidate to present to the rest of the class to explain why she or he should be elected. Then listen to the various candidates' statements and hold a mock election to elect two representatives.

For your file

Write a letter to the school council on a Year 8 issue (for example, the lack of a social area for Year 8 students at break times; the need to improve the provision of lockers and locker space for Year 8 students; the amount of bullying of Year 8s by older students), asking the school council to discuss the issue and take it up with the teaching staff.

The Henry Box School –
School Uniform

It is the policy of the school that all students in Years 7-11 wear the agreed uniform. Our school uniform helps to create a smart appearance, a sense of belonging from a common identity and a feeling of pride in The Henry Box School. The full uniform must be worn to and from school.

THE MAIN SCHOOL UNIFORM

School sweatshirt – this is central to our uniform and all students will wear these.

Trousers and skirts – black (skirts around the knee; trousers should be no longer than shoes to avoid danger of tripping and should not be of excessive width) and traditional style (not denim or cord)

Shirt – white formal "school shirt" (vests or T-shirts must not show at the neck, and shirts must be tucked in unless it is a fitted formal shirt with collar for girls)

Socks – plain dark or white

Tights – plain black

Shoes – black, plain, low heeled (no higher than 6cm) of a sensible design.

ADDITIONAL ITEMS

Outside coats – It is important that students have a coat which is warm and weatherproof and which is of a normal style. The school reserves the right not to accept a coat if it would give a poor impression of The Henry Box School. Unacceptable coats include leather, simulated leather, suede, denim, track suit tops and coats with offensive logos. Unacceptable coats will be confiscated and the student provided with a suitable coat for the day.

Scarves – these may be worn in poor weather conditions outdoors.

Hats – in the summer in sunny weather only, plain navy blue hats (non-woollen) are permitted. During the winter in cold weather only, woollen hats are allowed. Hats/caps may be worn outdoors only. A small designer logo is allowed but football hats or those with large logos are not permitted. If hats are worn inappropriately or are of an unacceptable design or colour, they will be confiscated.

Trainers – these may be worn during sporting activities or on the tennis courts or field during break and lunchtime or curricular activities that require them. They should not be worn around school or on the way to and from school.

Jewellery – students may wear a wristwatch, a flat ring, a crucifix or similar. One small ear stud per ear is allowed but studs in other parts of the body are not permitted. It is not permitted to have illegal items of jewellery covered by a plaster.

Hair Dye – only hair dyed a natural colour is permitted. If a student dyes their hair an unnatural/bright colour, they will be isolated from lessons or sent home until the hair is returned to a natural colour. The school reserves the right not to accept a hair style which may give a poor impression of the school.

Make-up – not allowed in Key Stage 3. In Key Stage 4 discreet make-up is allowed. Coloured nail varnish is not allowed.

In groups

Imagine that your school is currently revising its dress code. Compare your school's dress code with The Henry Box School's dress code. Suggest how you would like to alter your current Year 8 uniform requirements. Make notes of your views, then share your ideas in a class discussion.

Organising a social event

This page explains how your class can work together to organise a social event.

There are various types of social event you could organise:

An ice-skating trip

A theatre trip to a play, a concert or show

A trip to an international sports event

A Year 8 disco

A visit to a theme park

Planning the event

 In groups

Discuss your ideas for a social event. Then share your ideas in a class discussion and hold a vote to decide what type of social event your class would like to organise.

Make a list of all the jobs that will have to be done in order for the event to take place. Then, share your ideas and draw up a complete list of everything that needs to be done (see 8L's list, right).

A planning committee

Once you have decided on the event and listed the jobs to be done, appoint a planning committee. The advantage of having a planning committee is that you can arrange for it to meet regularly to check that everything has been done and to deal with any problems that may arise.

Reviewing the event

After the event, hold a class discussion. Talk about what went well, the problems you faced while organising it, and how you coped with them. What were the strengths and weaknesses of how you organised the event? What lessons did you learn? How would you do things differently, if you were to organise a similar event in the future?

8L Ice-Skating Trip

Checklist of tasks for planning committee

✓ Choose date and check school calendar to check that it doesn't clash with any other event.

✓ Contact ice-rink to check opening times, cost of entrance, skate hire and what refreshments are on sale.

✓ Contact bus company to check availability and cost of coach, and book coach.

✓ Advertise the trip and get people to sign up for it.

✓ Check Health and Safety Regulations to ensure that there are enough adults available to come on trip.

✓ Send out letter to inform parents of arrangements for trip.

✓ Arrange for collection of money to pay for the coach.

Planning a budget for your trip

The cost of the coach

The cost of a coach will vary depending on the size of the coach you require and how far the journey is, for example, from the school to the ice-rink. Also, different companies may charge different prices.

The 8L planning committee decided to get quotes from three different coach companies. They found that the cost of hiring a 29-seater or a 30-seater coach for the evening varied from £200 with one company to £240 with another company. One of the companies also asked for a £50 deposit when the booking was confirmed.

All three companies had a cancellation policy. For example, the Buzz-A-Bus company would charge 25% of the total cost of £200 i.e. £50, if the booking was cancelled 28 days before, rising to 100%, if the booking was cancelled on the day of the trip.

The committee worked out that if they booked a 29-seater coach for £200, they could charge everyone going on the trip £6.89. They decided to round up the charge to £7 per person and to give the extra £3 to the driver as a tip.

    Income from coach charge 29 x £7 = £203
    Expenditure on coach   £200
    Tip for driver   £3

The 8L committee asked the school council for a loan of £200 to pay for the coach, in case the trip had to be cancelled due to unforeseen circumstances. The committee had to agree to organise a fundraising event to raise money to repay the loan, if necessary.

Entrance to the ice-rink

The committee contacted the ice-rink and found that the entrance fee (including skate hire) varied according to the times of the sessions. The least expensive sessions were the early evening sessions when entrance fees for under 17s were £3.90. Entrance for the 2-hour Friday night disco was £6.10 with no reductions for under 17s. When they asked about discounts for party bookings, they were told that for a party of 29 the entrance fee to the disco session would be reduced to £5.20.

After consulting with the rest of the class, the committee chose to go to the disco evening and sent out a letter saying that the trip would cost £12.20 - £7 for the coach and £5.20 for entrance to the ice-rink.

In groups

Work out a budget for a class trip, similar to 8L's ice-skating trip

If someone is ill and unable to go on a trip after they have paid for a place, would you refund their money? Discuss the arguments for and against offering a refund.

Facts and opinions

Whenever you discuss an issue, it is important to listen to other people's views, to consider their arguments and, if they are convincing, to change your mind about what you think.

In order to be able to judge the strength of other people's arguments, you need to be able to distinguish whether what they are saying is a **fact** or an **opinion**.

A **fact** is a true statement. It can be about an event or thing that is known to have happened or about something which can be shown to be true by experience or observation. For example:

> *" Many animals which are seriously ill and dying suffer a lot of pain. "*

An **opinion** is a judgement or belief. It is a statement of a point of view based on what a person thinks and feels. For example:

> *" Dying animals should be put down. "*

When someone is explaining the reasons why they hold an opinion, they often use a fact to support their view. For example:

> *" Dying animals should be put down, because many animals which are seriously ill and dying suffer a lot of pain. "*

Forming your opinion

Before you take part in any discussion ...

Find out the facts. For example, by reading articles on the subject or looking for information in the library and on the Internet. Check that any information you already have is correct and up to date.

Identify what the main issue is and what different opinions people have. Note down the arguments that are used for and against a particular point of view and any facts and examples used to support those arguments.

Decide what your opinion is. Make a list of arguments why you hold that opinion.

During the discussion ...

Listen to what other people have to say. Note down any new arguments that people introduce or any key facts which you learn from them.

If you find other people's opinions convincing, be prepared to alter your own opinion. However, if you think you are right, don't be pressurised into changing your opinion just because other people don't agree with you. Each of you has a right to their own opinion and you should agree to differ.

In pairs

Study the list of statements (below) and decide which are facts and which are opinions.

1 Tongue-piercing can cause infections.

2 Body-piercing improves your looks.

3 Animals should be left to die completely natural deaths.

4 Vets can advise you whether or not your pet is terminally ill.

5 There are a number of decisions which 12-year-olds cannot make for themselves.

6 Twelve-year-old children are good at making decisions.

7 There is too much violence in television programmes.

8 Some popular cartoon series contain scenes of violence.

9 Many roads get congested around the time that schools start.

10 Pupils who live within three miles of their school should always walk or cycle to school.

Body-piercing – what's your verdict?

Should body-piercing be banned?

NO says Kit, 16

'I can't believe everyone makes such a big deal about body-piercing when it's not hurting anyone except the person who gets it done.

It looks good and original. The trouble is parents completely freak when you say you want one because they think of people with piercings all over their body. I would never do that. All I want is a single stud over my eye which is totally different.

It annoys me that people with piercings get a bad reputation, too. People think that you're a thug. That's stupid. Quite a few of my friends have had their belly pierced or a stud put in their tongue. It doesn't make them bad people; it doesn't change their personality.

Safety is something I think about. But unless you're stupid enough to do one yourself, the risks are low. All the proper shops are hygienic so you're more likely to get knocked down by a bus than get an infection.'

YES says Kit's mother, Candy

'I know that piercing is fashionable but it looks so ugly and primitive. I don't want people to judge Kit badly because he's got a piece of metal sticking out of his face.

If Kit has an eyebrow pierced he'll have to look at it every day of his life – and I'm worried that he'll regret that later on. It's all very well saying that it's not forever. Even if he took it out he could be left with a bad scar.

I don't even want to think about the health risks. Kit tells me piercing shops sterilise their equipment, but there are no guarantees. I'm not stupid. I know there are still a lot of places that are really unhygienic. It's easy to get an infection from a dirty piercing gun.'

Sickening sight!

I think the whole idea of body-piercing is quite sick! Who would want to walk down the street with their nose, eyebrow and other body parts pierced?

Ear-piercing is fine but some people go way over the top by piercing other parts of their body. Several girls in my school think that having a pierced belly button is cool. No chance!

❝ There is no official age limit under which you are not allowed to do body-piercing, but we suggest members use their own ethics and morals. We would support some sort of legislation or guidelines. ❞

– Zoe Rockliffe, secretary of the European Professional Piercing Association

● On your own

Study the information and views about body-piercing given in the articles on this page. Make notes on the facts and opinions they contain. Form your own opinion about body-piercing and identify the arguments you are going to use to support your opinion.

In groups

Discuss your views on body-piercing.

Dentists warn of piercing perils

Tongue-piercing can cause infections, interfere with breathing, damage the teeth and lead to speech impediments, say dentists.

'People having tongue-piercings are putting not just their oral health, but their general health at risk – and we strongly advise people not to,' said Dr Geoff Craig of the British Dental Association.

'If people insist on having piercings, they should ensure that the equipment is sterilised properly and that the stud is made of gold, surgical steel or titanium.'

For your file

Write a short statement expressing your opinion on body-piercing, explaining why you have or have not changed your mind as a result of the discussion.

Debating the issue

A debate is a formal discussion in which two opposing arguments are put forward.

The rules of debating

The meeting is opened by the **chair** – the person who controls the meeting and decides who will speak and when. To start the meeting, the chair reads out the **motion** to be debated. The motion is the viewpoint which people will argue for or against. It is presented in a formal way which begins: 'This house believes that …'

The debate begins with a speech in favour of the motion. The person who speaks first in favour of the motion is called the **proposer**.

Then there is a speech against the motion by a person called the **opposer**.

The chair then declares the motion **open to the floor**. This means that anyone in the audience may now speak either for or against the motion. Anyone who wishes to speak raises their hand, and the chair asks them to speak in turn.

There are then two further speeches – one in favour of and one against the motion. The people who give these speeches are called **seconders**.

After a suitable time to allow as many people as possible to express their views, the chair invites the main speakers to **sum up**. The opposer gives a summary of the main arguments why people should vote against the motion, and the proposer gives a summary of the main arguments why they should vote for the motion.

A **vote** is then organised. The chair reads out the motion and asks 'all those in favour' to raise their hands. They are counted, and then 'all those against' are asked to raise their hands. After they are counted, the chair asks those who wish to **abstain** to raise their hands and the abstentions are counted. (You may wish to abstain for a number of reasons, either because you cannot make up your mind or because you do not agree with either of the views people have expressed.)

Organise your own debate

Either choose your own motion or organise a debate on one of these motions:

1 This house believes that all animals have the right to die naturally.

2 This house believes that children should be allowed to wear what they like to school.

3 This house believes that the monarchy is out of date and should be abolished.

The chair announces the **result** of the vote and declares that the motion has 'been carried' or 'passed' (the house agrees with motion) or 'defeated' (the house disagrees with the motion).

Tips on Writing a Speech

Grab their attention *Make sure you start with a statement or question that will capture the audience's attention.* For example:
'What's wrong with eating meat? 90% of us do. So why should we feel guilty?'

Use facts and statistics *Support your statements with statistics and examples. This strengthens your arguments.* For example:
'As many as 90% of battery hens are unable to walk properly.'

Include lists of three *Statements which list things in threes are more likely to hold the audience's attention and stick in their minds.* For example:
'Vegetarianism is cruelty-free, environmentally friendly and healthy.'

Use alliteration *A statement which includes a number of words starting with the same letter is likely to be more memorable.* For example:
'It's time to stop the senseless slaughter.'

Refer to personal experiences *This suggests you really know what you are talking about.* For example:
'I've seen pictures of calves, only a few days old …'

Include questions *These can have a dramatic effect, particularly if they are questions that do not require an answer (these are called rhetorical questions).* For example:
'Isn't it obvious that a meat-free diet is better?'

Involve the audience *Addressing the audience directly can help to get them on your side.* For example:
'How would you like to spend your life cooped up in a cage?'

'Set them up and knock them down' *This is a particularly effective way of undermining the opposition's arguments.* For example:
'What I can't stand about most so-called vegetarians is their hypocrisy. They claim that they don't eat meat to stop animals suffering, yet they go on eating other animal products like eggs and cheese.'

End emphatically *Make sure you end your speech on a high note.* For example:
'Whenever you eat meat you're taking the food out of someone else's mouth. If everyone in the world was to become a vegetarian, there'd be enough food for everybody.'

Writing a speech

There are a number of techniques you can use when writing a speech in order to make it more effective. The advice above is from a helpsheet which a teacher gave to a class who were going to debate the motion 'This house believes that people who aren't vegetarians are selfish and cruel.'

 In pairs

Research the topic, to find out the facts and what the arguments are for and against the issue that is being debated. Then form your opinions. Tell each other which side of the argument you support and draft your speech.

Show your speech to your partner and each make any suggestions you can think of to improve it.

Some young people enter into sexual relationships and have sex without thinking about the consequences. The aim of this unit is to make you aware of what is involved in having a sexual relationship and of the steps you can take to avoid an unwanted pregnancy and to avoid catching a sexually transmitted infection.

Sex and Contraception ...
Your Questions Answered

1 What is the right age to have sex?

In Britain it is illegal for a boy to have sex with a girl under the age of 16.

We all know that some girls are very mature at 16 and some are still years away from forming serious relationships. The choice and risks are yours to take, but what's revealing is that the more teenagers know about sex and relationships, the longer they wait to make love. Young people in Holland (who are usually given frank sex education from an early age and find it easier than us Brits to talk openly with parents and teachers) start having sex an average of two years after we do.

Make up your own mind, don't bow to peer pressure and get all the facts and info you need to make informed and safe decisions about your own sex life – then you'll know when the time is right.

2 Who should I talk to about contraception?

The first person you should speak to is the person you're planning to have sex with. This should be something he has to worry about too. If you're counting on acting as a couple then you should sort out contraception together. That could mean he comes along to the doctor's with you to lend a bit of support or maybe he's the one who buys the condoms.

3 What if I'm underage and I want contraceptive advice?

Most doctors will be understanding about what you want and will treat your case in confidence. You can double check about confidentiality beforehand if you don't want your parents to know that you need birth control (see question 4). What you'll find is that most medical staff would rather see you taking a sensible view towards contraception than coming in a few months later asking for a pregnancy test.

4 Can my doctor tell my parents I'm having sex?

This is still very much up to the individual doctor, but most GPs now agree that young people under 16 can see them for contraceptive advice without parental consent. If you are not sure your doctor offers this service then you can phone reception and ask if he or she will give under-16s this sort of treatment. If you don't feel confident enough to go there then try making an appointment at a family planning clinic or at Brook.

5 Is the pill foolproof?

The pill is one of the most reliable forms of contraception, but only if you follow the instructions on the enclosed leaflet very carefully. If you skip pills or vary the times when they are taken then you may reduce the effectiveness.

Contraceptive injections are another method that some more forgetful pill-takers are turning to. They are given a painless injection in their backside every 12 weeks and are protected until their next appointment at the clinic.

6 What is emergency contraception?

Some people still refer to emergency contraception as the morning-after pill, which is confusing because it can be taken up to 72 hours after unprotected sex has taken place. If you think you need emergency contraception, make an appointment with your doctor or phone a clinic.

Natural methods of preventing unwanted pregnancies

The trouble with natural methods of avoiding an unwanted pregnancy is that they are either unsuitable for teenagers or not reliable.

I'm worried about protection

'I'm 13 and I'm going steady with a boy. Last weekend we were in his bedroom and we ended up on the bed. We would have gone all the way if I hadn't said I had my period. I'm very worried about contraception. I overheard him talking to his best mate saying that we were going to have sex and that we didn't need to use contraception. I don't know what to do. I'm scared to say anything, but I don't want to end up pregnant.'

Tricia Kreitman says:

Having sex without a condom or any other form of contraception means one thing – you get pregnant, probably quite quickly.

I don't think you should have sex with him at all. This boy's a real idiot and he's bragging to his friends that he's going to get you into bed. Presumably he sees not wearing a condom as some kind of macho statement, whereas in reality it's stupidity and cowardice.

I'm sorry but I think you're both too young to have sex and the very fact you can't discuss contraception illustrates this. Legally you're still three years under the age of consent and, if he's older than you, he could get into real trouble.

But more important, I can see that you are likely to get hurt. I don't think this boy's worth the bother because he sees you as a trophy or something to brag about rather than someone he's in love with. Please give it more time and don't do anything that you'll regret.

The rhythm method

This works on the principle that there are certain days within your cycle when you can have sex without getting pregnant. It's not suitable for young people because you need to have extremely regular periods to work out your fertile and infertile days. It also means you have to plan sex. On top of all this, this method does not protect you from HIV and STIs (sexually transmitted infections).

Withdrawal

Not a reliable form of contraception. Withdrawal is when a boy removes his penis from a girl's vagina before he ejaculates. It's a useless method because sperm can and does leak out before ejaculation. It's impossible to control this – so don't believe any boy who says he can stop it happening.

🔳 In groups

'Setting the age of consent at 16 is wrong.' Discuss this view. What are the arguments for and against:
a) raising the age of consent to 18; b) lowering the age of consent to 14?

Sexual rights and responsibilities

In any sexual relationship you have rights and responsibilities.

Your Sexual Responsibilities

1 You should always consider the feelings of your partner.

The key to a happy relationship is considering the feelings of your partner. When you are sensitive to his or her moods, likes and dislikes, you can build trust and relaxation between you. So if your partner is upset about something and wants to talk rather than kiss, put your own wishes aside for the moment and tend to his or her needs.

2 You should never pressurise someone to have sex.

Pressurising someone to have sex is pointless because no amount of pressure is going to create desire where there wasn't any before. If you are a boy, you should never try to force a girl to have sex with you. Even if you genuinely think a girl intends to make love and are surprised when she won't, you shouldn't pressurise her.

To use any kind of advantage or physical pressure to force a person to have sex is assault.

3 You should respect your partner.

Sex can make you feel vulnerable, especially when you're new to it. That is why good sexual relations require trust between the partners. If a boy or girl has told you secrets, declared love for you, or made some kind of love with you, you should never make fun of him or her for it. When people have been intimate with you like that they have made themselves vulnerable to you. Don't betray them.

4 You should share the responsibility for birth control and sexual health with your partner.

Part of respecting someone and being considerate of his or her feelings is being concerned over the consequences of your sexual relationship together. With the increase of sexual diseases, especially AIDS, you have a right to know if your partner is healthy. And you have a responsibility to avoid sex if you have a sexual disease.

The responsibility for birth control also belongs to both partners.

Your Sexual Rights

1 You have a right to enjoy sex.

When there's a lot of talk about sexual abuse, it's sometimes hard to remember that sex itself is a beautiful, natural experience – or it should be.

2 You have a right to wait until you're ready for sex.

One of the main ways to guarantee that you will enjoy sex is to wait until you're ready. Don't make yourself start sex before you really want to just to please a partner or keep up with the crowd.

3 You always have a right to say no.

Your right to say no never changes whatever the circumstances. If someone's spent money on you, taken you out, or given you presents, you don't owe him even as much as a kiss. Even if you've promised to make love and then changed your mind, you have a right to say no. Your body is not a bargaining chip and you are not for sale.

4 You have a right to be respected.

No one should tell you he doesn't respect you because of your sexual activities, or pressurise you because of them.

5 You have a right to say yes to some sexual activities and no to others.

Just because you've become physically intimate with someone doesn't mean you have to do anything you don't want. If you've almost gone all the way but haven't, you aren't obliged to. If a boy tells you that you've gone too far to stop, don't believe him.

This applies to boys too. You have as much right as anyone to stop when you want and refuse what you don't want.

Where to go for advice

If you need help or advice on contraception or sexual health, there should be a clinic in your area that runs sessions for young people. Ask at a health centre or look in the phone book under 'Family Planning'.

Confidential helplines
• Brook 0800 0185 023 • Childline 0800 1111

What is acceptable in a sexual relationship?

In groups

People have different views about what is acceptable in a sexual relationship. On your own study the list (below) and decide which types of behaviour you think are acceptable and which are unacceptable. Then share your views in a group discussion.

1 To do things to please your boy/girlfriend.

2 To tell your friends all about what you and your partner do together.

3 To stop seeing a friend if your boy/girlfriend doesn't like them.

4 To have a relationship with someone of a different religion.

5 To lie to your parent(s) or friends about where you are going and what you are doing.

6 To have sex without being in love.

7 To tell lies to your boy/girlfriend, if you think the truth might hurt them.

8 To start having sex because one person wants to.

9 To hit each other.

10 To argue a lot.

11 To disagree about issues.

12 To go out with your friends without your boy/girlfriend.

13 To be attracted to other people while you are in a relationship.

14 To be sexually faithful to one another.

15 To let one partner take full responsibility for taking precautions.

16 To change your mind about doing something that you have made a promise to do.

Sex Myths

Everybody's doing it

Everybody's talking about it, but not everybody's doing it. If you are surrounded by friends who boast about having sex, take what they say with a pinch of salt. For starters, sex isn't something to show off about. It's a private thing between two people. Girls and boys who feel the need to tell all to everyone are usually trying to hide something.

Having sex means you are grown-up

Sex doesn't have anything to do with being grown-up, mature or adult. In fact, lots of adults make terrible mistakes when it comes to sex. They rush into things, and live to regret it in the same way that you or I might do. Being older doesn't mean you're wiser, in the same way that doing adult things doesn't make you an adult.

Sex strengthens a relationship

Sex only strengthens a relationship that's already strong. That means a relationship where you know and care about each other, where you've discussed things, and taken the right precautions. If you haven't done these things, sex will only weaken your relationship.

Britain and the European Union

The European Union (EU) is a group of countries who have joined together to co-operate on economic and political issues. In 2008 there were 27 member states. The main aim of the EU is to create lasting peace and prosperity for all its citizens.

Applicant for membership
EU members 2004
New members 2007

0 — 400 km

HOW IT BEGAN

The foundations of the EU were laid at the end of the Second World War (1939–45). This war was the third conflict in 70 years between two of Europe's biggest countries – France and Germany.

After the war, two Frenchmen – Jean Monnet and Robert Schuman – said there would only be lasting peace in Europe if Germany and France could learn to be friends. They decided that one way of achieving this would be to take two industries important to both countries – steel and coal – and hand over control of them to a body run by neither France nor Germany.

Other countries were also invited to join the new body when it was set up in 1951, and four did so – Italy, Belgium, Luxembourg and the Netherlands. In 1957 all six nations signed the Treaty of Rome and formed the European Economic Community (EEC). This created what is known as a Customs Union in which the six countries agreed not to put special taxes, known as tariffs, on goods imported from the other five member states.

Until this point, it was possible for Germany, for example, to put tariffs on French wine, making it dearer in German shops and therefore more difficult to sell.

Why didn't Britain join from the start?

In 1951 Britain still had strong ties with countries outside Europe. It directly controlled a number of colonies in Africa and the Caribbean, and relied on former colonies such as Australia and New Zealand for cheap food. Britain felt that its food would become more expensive and its links with colonies and former colonies would be weakened by membership of Europe. There were also fears that Britain would be giving up the right to make its own decisions.

By the 1960s, Britain changed its mind and applied to join the EEC. But the application was turned down twice by France because its president, Charles de Gaulle, thought Britain would be disruptive. However, in 1973, after de Gaulle's death, Britain did finally become a member along with the Republic of Ireland and Denmark. There was still dispute over whether our government at the time was right to make the decision, so a special vote – or referendum – was held in 1975. The whole nation voted, and around two thirds said Britain should remain part of the EEC.

The development of the EU

★ **1981** Greece joins the EEC.

★ **1986** Spain and Portugal join the EEC.

★ **1987** The Single European Act is passed. Member states agree to establish a single market by the end of 1992.

★ **1992** The Maastricht Treaty is signed. Members agree to discuss future co-operation and to review their political, economic and cultural links. A decision is made to introduce a single currency (see page 79) by the beginning of 1999. But the UK negotiated an 'opt-out' clause allowing it to decide whether to join at a later stage.

★ **1993** The single market is set up. The EEC becomes the EU.

★ **1995** Austria, Finland and Sweden join the EU.

★ **1997** The Treaty of Amsterdam made preparations for the EU to be enlarged.

★ **1999** The single currency is introduced.

★ **2004** Ten new member states joined (see map above).

★ **2007** Romania and Bulgaria joined.

The Single Market

By 1 January 1993, the then 12 EU countries were part of a Single Market where they could exchange goods without long and expensive delays at the frontiers and make it easier for people to move around to other countries – this is often called the free movement of goods, capital, services and people.

The idea is that companies can buy, sell and invest in any EU country without having to go through checks, pay VAT in each country or go through long and expensive import/export formalities at the frontier – saving a lot of time, red tape and money. This also means that more and more products are available from all round the EU in our shops, and at cheaper prices.

🔠 In groups

Discuss how the EEC was set up and why Britain did not join until 1973.

Explain what the Single Market is and what advantages there are for the EU countries which belong to it.

🔠 In groups

What do you see as the advantages and disadvantages of Britain's membership of the European Union? Are you for or against continued membership of the EU? Give your reasons.

Organise a debate on the motion: 'This house believes that Britain should withdraw from the EU.'

Should Britain remain in the EU?

Since the UK joined the EEC in 1973 there has been an on-going debate about whether it should remain a member.

A YouGov survey published in 2009 asked people: what is the ideal relationship between Britain and the EU?

* 14% said Britain should withdraw.
* 48% said Britain should have a looser relationship i.e. be in Europe, but not run by Europe.
* 22% said Britain should remain a full member on current terms.

Supporters

Supporters of the European movement argue that the UK's trade with Europe has grown enormously since the UK joined the EEC. 59% of UK exports are sold to other EU countries. Withdrawing from the EU would have a dramatic impact on our trade. It could affect our economy to such a degree that people's standard of living might fall.

They also point to the fact that you can travel freely within EU countries, with few of the border controls that other countries have in place. Also, any citizen of

Europe can work in any of the member states.

Critics

Critics of the EU, such as the UK Independence Party (UKIP), argue that the EU is wasteful and inefficient. They point out that about £1 billion a year (1.4% of the EU budget) is lost through fraud. They argue that Britain would be just as prosperous economically if more of its trade was done with other countries, such as the USA.

Opponents of the EU say that too many decisions are taken in Brussels rather than in London. For example, they are strongly opposed to proposals that taxation in EU countries should be harmonised. They say that belonging to the EU undermines Britain's national sovereignty, because European law has supremacy over national law.

How does the EU affect you?

Being a citizen of the EU makes it easier for you to travel, study or work in Europe. It also protects your rights, your health and your safety and helps to provide you with a good standard of living.

Your standard of living

As a European citizen you should enjoy a higher standard of living. The 25 countries in the EU work together to develop their economies so that people in all the member states will benefit. For example, money is given to projects in the poorer regions so that companies can make a profit and create jobs. In your area you might see a new bridge, a new motorway or a new business centre being built. EU money is given to regions where there is industrial decline, rural depopulation and high unemployment to pay for the development of the infrastructure.

Your human rights

The European Union is committed to the elimination of racism and other forms of discrimination both within its borders and throughout the world.

The EU also supports equal opportunities for women. The 1997 Treaty of Amsterdam expressly banned discrimination on grounds of sex in all member states.

The European Commission on Human Rights exists to see that human rights are upheld in all EU countries. If you feel that your human rights have been violated, you can write to the Commission. It will then decide whether to pass your case to the European Court of Human Rights.

Your career opportunities

Special programmes provide opportunities for you to travel, study and/or gain work experience in another member state. Under EU rules the qualifications you gain in one country must, in general, be recognised in other countries. You also have the right to receive the same job opportunities, terms and conditions of employment, or to set up a business anywhere in the EU.

Your rights as a consumer

Your rights as a consumer are protected by a set of rules that apply to shops throughout the EU. For example, foods must be clearly labelled to show their ingredients and how much they weigh and measure.

Items such as toys and electrical goods have to meet very strict safety regulations. Those which have passed the tests are marked with the CE mark.

You can buy goods produced in EU countries without having to pay the extra costs or duty that is usually put on things which are imported from other countries. This gives you more choice at reasonable prices.

Your right to travel

Being a citizen of the EU makes it easier to travel abroad. Your burgundy coloured European passport makes it easy to cross borders and you can go through the 'blue exit' at ports and airports, without having to make any declaration to customs, provided that you are carrying only goods for your personal use.

If you are ill while you are in a member state, you can receive medical attention just as you would at home. You simply have to fill in a form called an E111 which you can obtain from your nearest main post office, before you go abroad.

In groups

Discuss what you learn from this page about how being a citizen of Europe affects you. What effect do you think it would have on you if Britain were to withdraw from the EU?

What the EU does to protect the environment

- To combat pollution of the air you breathe EU rules have been set to reduce the levels of pollutants coming from vehicle emissions and factories. In December 2007 the EU pledged to force car manufacturers to cut emissions by at least 20% in the next five years.

- To conserve resources EU leaders have agreed that 20% of the EU's energy should come from renewable sources by 2020. For example, 10% of road fuel is to be composed of biofuel by 2020.

- EU rules set minimum water quality standards for the water you drink.

- EU rules ensure that bathing water is clean. When you go on holiday look out for the European Blue Flag for beaches. This is awarded to the cleanest beaches in Europe.

- Regulations have been introduced to reduce noise emissions from motor vehicles and aircraft and to protect workers in the workplace.

- The EU encourages the safe disposal and reuse of waste, especially nuclear materials, and safety measures for the transport of chemicals and other dangerous substances.

- The EU has introduced a labelling system which enables consumers to know whether the products they buy are bad for the environment. When your parents buy a new washing machine, for example, they should look for the 'ECO-label' which tells you which products cause least damage to the environment.

- Farmers are being made to use fewer pesticides and to employ agricultural production methods which preserve the countryside.

- Money is given to local and regional areas in designated areas of conservation to protect wildlife and the countryside.

Your environment

The EU has been developing a series of Environmental Action Programmes. These are designed to make the environment in which you live safe and healthy.

In groups

List and discuss all the measures that Europe has taken so far to protect the environment. Suggest other things that you think the EU should do in order to protect the environment.

For your file

Imagine that you are standing as a candidate for the Green Party in a European election. Write a statement explaining: a) why you think protecting the environment is of the utmost importance, b) what issues you consider to be important, and c) what further measures you think the EU should take to protect the environment.

How is the European Union run?

The EU is run by five main institutions which, together with the European Council, make, interpret and monitor the laws of the European Union.

The European Council is a summit meeting of the heads of government of each member state. It meets four times a year to discuss policy and give overall direction to the EU's programme.

European institutions

The Council of The European Union

This is the EU's main decision-making body. It consists of one government minister from each member state. They discuss proposals for new laws put forward by the European Commission and ensure that national interests are considered. The Council is based in Brussels and each country takes a turn at holding its presidency, which changes every six months. In 2009 the presidency was shared between the Czech Republic and Sweden. It should not be confused with the European Council, which is the name given to the regular summit meetings of the heads of state or government from the member countries.

Each of the five main institutions has representatives from the 27 member states. So EU policies and decisions are made by UK representatives acting in consultation with representatives from the countries which are our partners in the EU.

The European Commission

There are 27 commissioners, who are appointed by the governments of the member countries. A new commission is appointed every five years. Each commissioner has responsibility for a particular area of policy. Once they have been appointed, commissioners are expected to act independently in the interests of all member states.

The Commission has four main roles: 1) it proposes new laws; 2) it manages and implements EU policies and the budget; 3) it enforces European law; 4) it represents the EU on the international stage.

The European Parliament

This meets in Strasbourg and consists of members who are elected from the 27 member states. Elections are held every five years, with elections in 2004, 2009 and 2014. Members of the European Parliament are known as MEPs and there are 78 MEPs from the UK.

MEPs have considerable powers. They are consulted on proposals for new laws, give their opinions, suggest amendments and in some cases make decisions jointly with the Council of Ministers, especially with regard to the budget (see page 81). The European Parliament can also dismiss the European Commission, if it feels that it is not operating as it should be.

The European Court of Justice

This sits in Luxembourg and there are 27 judges, one from each member state.

Its role is to interpret European laws and to decide whether actions are against European law. It has the power to rule against national governments which are breaking European laws. However, the European Court of Justice has no power to overturn decisions of British courts.

The European Court of Auditors

Its role is to monitor the financial management of the EU and to look after the interests of the EU's taxpaying citizens by checking that the EU's money is actually being used for the purposes for which it is intended. It also assists the European Parliament in checking the budget each year. The Court has 27 members, one for each country.

In groups

Discuss what you learn from this page about the institutions of the European Union. Where do you think the real power lies in the EU?

The Lowry Arts Centre, Salford Quays, in the former Manchester docks. With the help of the European Regional Development Fund, the Salford Quays have been transformed into a commercial, cultural and tourist centre, creating 4,000 jobs.

How European laws are made

The Commission forwards a proposal for a new EU law to the European Parliament.

The European Parliament discusses it, and perhaps amends it, then passes it back to the Commission.

The Commission drafts a firm proposal, which is sent to the Council of the European Union.

The Council makes suggestions and amendments, consulting their national parliaments. It then adopts a 'common position' on the proposal.

The 'common position' is considered by the European Parliament.

If the European Parliament approves, the Council adopts the proposal. Even if the Parliament rejects the proposal, the Council can adopt it as long as it is a unanimous decision.

EU regulations automatically become law in all member states. The EU can also pass 'directives' which tell member states to introduce a new law within a time limit.

In groups

Discuss what you learn from this page about **a)** how European laws are made, and **b)** how the EU raises money and how it spends it.

The EU budget

The EU budget in 2008 was £129.1 billion.

How the money was raised

★ 69% came from national contributions.

★ 15% came from VAT charged on goods and services by member states.

★ 15% came from customs duties on goods imported into the EU.

★ 1% came from other sources.

How the money was spent

★ 45% was spent on making the EU economy more competitive and dynamic and to increase the cohesion of the EU, i.e. by narrowing the gap between richer and poorer member states and regions.

★ 32% was spent on agriculture.

★ 11% was spent on rural development and the environment.

★ 6% was spent on administrative costs.

★ 6% was spent on world matters, such as overseas aid and external actions.

Developing the European Union

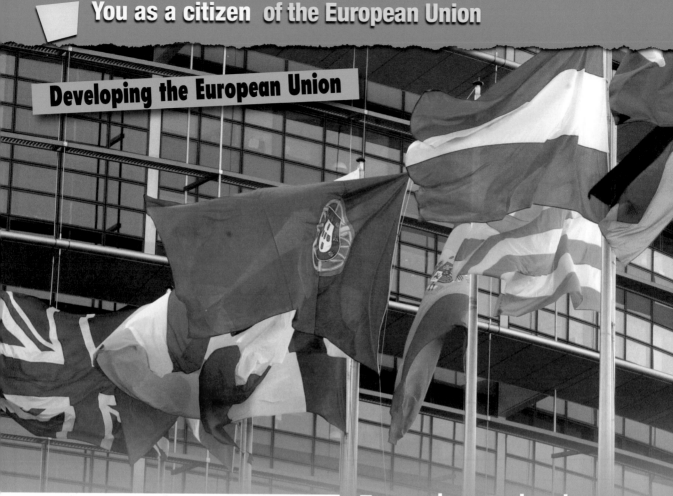

Any country in Europe can apply to join the EU. Turkey has submitted an application to join the EU (see map on page 76). Countries which apply to join the EU must meet certain requirements:

- Their system of government must be democratic.
- They must respect human rights.
- They must have a market economy that operates in the same way as the economies of existing EU member countries.

The EU has promised the Balkan countries that they can all join once the conditions are met. Croatia and Macedonia are already officially labelled as 'candidates' for membership.

'Any European country which applies for membership and meets the criteria should be accepted into the EU.' Say why you agree or disagree with this view.

Discuss the arguments for and against a federal Europe.

Towards a Federal Europe?

Some politicians want the members of the EU to develop much closer political links. They want to see taxes harmonised and a common foreign policy adopted. They think the EU should develop into a political union, in which each state, while retaining its national government, would increasingly operate as one of a federation of states in a 'United States of Europe'.

They are in favour of reducing the rights of member states to veto proposals on key issues. They support the changes introduced in the Treaty of Lisbon in 2007, whereby countries agreed to give up the veto in several key areas, including social security, foreign policy, trade and terrorism prevention.

Anti-federalists see closer political union as a threat to national sovereignty and national identity. They do not want to see the European Union become too powerful and fear that it could become dominated by the countries with the strongest economies. They think that in such a large political body individual citizens would have too little influence and that there would be too much bureaucracy and centralisation. They argue that the veto should be retained in many areas including taxation, defence, and social security.

The single currency

The idea of the single currency is to have one currency for countries within the EU. The aim is to make it easier and less costly for businesses to do trade. When you have different currencies, you have to pay something every time you change your money into another currency. Transferring money also takes time and causes delays. Besides, you can never be sure how much your money is going to be worth from day to day, as the rate of exchange varies.

The single currency, known as the **euro**, was introduced in 1999. Eleven countries joined the euro (making the euro zone): Germany, France, Italy, Spain, Netherlands, Belgium, Austria, Finland, Portugal, Ireland and Luxembourg. The British government decided not to join because it did not consider that the economic circumstances were right. It therefore delayed making a final decision on whether or not Britain should join.

A YouGov survey published in 2009 asked people: how would you vote in a referendum on whether Britain should join the euro? 24% said they would vote to join. 64% said they would vote against joining. 12% said they didn't know/would not vote.

Should Britain join the euro?

YES ✔

Having the same currency will mean we will be able to understand the exact amount we are spending when abroad. Instead of going into a shop in France, for example, and having to mentally convert euros into pounds, the price tag will be in euros.

The prices on some expensive goods – especially cars – vary considerably across Europe, and are often more expensive in Britain. A single currency would expose price differences (often amounting to thousands of pounds) and force retailers to cut their prices in order to compete.

We don't want to be left out – or behind. The euro zone countries are likely to form a powerful economic and political alliance from which Britain would be excluded. This would mean Britain having less influence over decisions made by the European Union which directly affect our everyday lives.

NO ✘

Joining the euro is a once-and-for-all step. There is no going back. It would mean abolishing the pound for ever.

Although the Government says it will judge whether Britain should join on economic grounds, it is also very much a political decision. Do we really want to be part of a process that could eventually lead to a single European country – a 'United States of Europe'? Or do we want to retain our national identity and independence?

Europe sells more to Britain than it buys – so it would certainly not be to their advantage to shut Britain out of a so-called single market.

⚏ In groups

Do you think Britain should join the euro? Discuss the arguments for and against Britain joining the single currency.

For your file

Write an email to a newspaper or magazine stating your views on the single currency issue.

Different types of business

Businesses vary in size from small businesses owned and run by one person to large national and multi-national companies employing tens of thousands of people in many different companies.

Working for yourself

When you work for yourself you are called a 'sole trader'. You work on your own and are responsible for your own business. This can be very risky. If your costs get out of control, you could lose a lot of money. On the other hand, if you make a lot of money you get to keep all of the profit.

It can be difficult to raise the money to start the business. Banks are less keen to lend money to sole traders. This is because of the high rate of failures. Of each three new businesses started each year, two will fail. It is very easy to lose all of your money. This is known as going bankrupt.

If your business goes bankrupt, you are personally responsible for all the money owed to other people. This money is known as debts. You may have to sell your car and even your house, if as a sole trader your business is bankrupt.

Sole traders are very common in the service industries. Examples include shopkeepers, writers and hairdressers.

Partnerships

In a partnership, you share the risk. Between two and twenty people run the business.

They own it, control it, provide the starting money for it and share the profits from it.

To form a partnership you sign a special agreement called a Deed of Partnership.

Because more than one person is involved, it is easier to raise money for this type of business. But if the business fails, all the partners have to pay off the debts.

One advantage of working in a partnership is that different people can provide different skills. For example, Trevor worked on his own as a plumber and his sister Shereen worked as an electrician. They formed a partnership with their friend Amrit, a carpenter, to do household maintenance work. They called themselves Household Solutions.

Azam owns and runs a newsagent's shop.

Working for a company

Working for a company removes a lot of the risks. Instead of sharing in the profits, you will be paid a salary by the company. This is how many people work in the UK. However, your salary will usually be fixed. This means that even if the company is very successful, you will still receive the same amount of money.

Also, the company may fail. When the retailers Woolworths collapsed in 2008 thousands of people lost their jobs.

W H Smiths are a national company selling books, magazines and stationery

Shell is a multi-national company with business interests all over the world

Working in the public, private or voluntary sector

If you own your own company, or work for a private company, this is known as working in the private sector. The rewards in the private sector are large, but the risks are the greatest.

Alternatively, you may work for the Government, for example, as a nurse, doctor or teacher. This is known as working in the public sector. Public sector wages tend to be lower than in the private sector. However, the risks are less, as the government is always going to need staff for public services, for example, in hospitals and in schools.

A third option is working in the voluntary sector. This can involve working as a volunteer, or as a paid member of staff, for some sort of charity. For example, Tina worked as a nurse until she retired. Now she works as a volunteer for Age Concern, which helps and supports older people.

In groups

On your own, list the advantages and disadvantages of **a)** working for yourself **b)** working for a company. Then share your views in a group discussion.

Discuss what the differences are between working in the private sector and working in the public sector. Which sector provides more job security? Which provides the most rewards? Which is more risky?

How is a firm organised

In order for a business to be successful, it must perform a variety of different tasks. This means that different people play different roles in the business.

Here is an example of a small business that produces goods.

Production

Production makes the goods that are being sold. It tries to do this as cheaply as possible. This ensures that costs are low, so that profits can be high.

Research

Research and development (or R&D) researches new products for sale in the future. For example, a toymaker develops new toys and games. They work with customers to find out what new games they like playing, and what would sell the best.

Public relations

The image of a company can greatly affect its sales. This affects its profits. Public relations ensure that the image of the company is presented in the best possible way. This involves communicating with customers, management and the company workforce, as well as the media.

Sales and marketing

Sales and marketing are responsible for selling as many of the goods as possible. It advertises the goods for sale and sets sales targets to be reached.

Support services

Every company needs cleaners, food for the staff to eat, secretaries, electricity and computers. These are all known as support services.

Finance and accounting

These departments make sure that costs are kept low and revenue (income) is as high as possible.

Management

The group of managers which controls the overall management of the company is called the Board of Directors. At the head of this group is the Managing Director of the company.

In pairs

Research a local business to find out how it is organised. It could be a manufacturing firm, a shop or a business that provides a service of some kind. Contact the firm to find out if it has a website you could visit and what leaflets (if any) they produce about the firm. Then arrange to visit the firm to interview someone about how it is organised. Before your visit, make a list of questions about the information you want to obtain. Then, after the visit, draft a report to present to the rest of your class.

Social entrepreneurs

An entrepreneur is a person who creates a new business. Social entrepreneurs try to create new businesses that do not just operate for profit. They also have some sort of social aim. This might be:

- To create more jobs in an area of high unemployment.
- To recycle more local rubbish so it doesn't end up in the ground.
- To educate young people about the dangers of binge drinking.
- To provide a service missing in the local community (e.g. meals on wheels)
- To provide training opportunities for young people.

A social enterprise — GREEN WORKS

A business with social aims is called a social enterprise. Green Works is a social enterprise which collects unwanted office furniture from big companies like Marks and Spencer and recycles it to sell at a discount.

Green Works charges a fee to take desks, chairs, tables and coat-stands to one of its six London warehouses. These are sold to schools, colleges, charities, housing associations and small businesses.

'I'm here to stop furniture filling up landfill, not to boost profits so that I can holiday in Barbados,' says the founder Colin Crooks.

Since 2000, his business has taken more than 60,000 tonnes of furniture that would have ended up in landfill.

Meanwhile, schools, colleges, charities and small businesses have saved around £2.5 million buying from Green Works.

Green Works's motto is 'Waste nothing'. Even damaged goods are given a new purpose, with chipboard sent off to a specialist plant to be converted into fuel pellets for Belgian and German power plants.

In groups

What kind of social enterprise would benefit your local community? Imagine that a local person has offered to fund the setting up of a business that would benefit the community. Share your ideas for a social enterprise and choose one of them to present to the rest of the class. Then, as a class, vote to decide which group has the best proposal.

For your file

Write a statement saying why you agree or disagree with the social enterprise that the class chose as the best proposal.

Financing a business

Businesses need money for a variety of reasons. Firstly, they need money to buy the raw materials it takes to make the goods they manufacture. They will also need money to rent or buy premises, for example for a factory and for the machinery required to make the goods. These are known as fixed costs.

The business will also need to pay money for its workers who make the goods. These are known as the workforce. Heating, lighting and electricity will also need to be paid for. The factory will need cleaning, which also costs money. The goods will need promoting through sales and marketing. All of these are known as variable costs.

Finally, a firm may need money to pay off a bank loan that was taken out to start up the business, or to pay shareholders a percentage of the profits.

The Money-go-round

Outside investment

Money

In exchange for

Used to pay for

Resources:
Machines
Wages for labour
Raw materials

Customers

Sold to

To produce

Goods/
services

In groups

You are partners in a small manufacturing business which is doing well. You need to raise money to buy more equipment and to take on more staff. Discuss how you could raise the money. Which of the four options would you choose? Give reasons for your views.

Four ways of raising money

1 The first way of raising money is to put your own money into the business. This is easy to do, but very risky. If your business fails, you will lose all of your money.

2 A second way of raising money is to borrow the money from a bank. This is known as a loan. However, you have to pay more money back than you borrowed. The extra amount you pay is known as interest.

3 A third way is to invite several people to help run your business. Each of these people is known as a partner. The partners each put an amount of their money into the business, so they end up sharing the risk. But if the business is a success they also share the profits.

4 Finally, you can sell parts of your business in order to raise money. This is done by dividing your business into shares. For example, if you had 100 shares in your business, each person who owned one share would own 1% of the business. These people are known as shareholders.

In return for investing money, shareholders expect a share of the profits. This is known as a dividend. If the value of the business goes up, shareholders can sell their shares for more money as well.

Risk and profit

Just because you have raised the money, it doesn't mean that the business will be a success. Unexpected things can happy. Prices can rise, demand can fall (people don't want your goods or services so much), competitors can take away your share of the market or illness can hit the employees of the company, creating extra costs.

Jonathan's story

Jonathan runs a transport business, moving goods from one place to another. He has ten lorries which do this. A major part of Jonathan's running costs is petrol.

In 2006 Jonathan was making a healthy profit. However, petrol was then only 80p per litre. But because of problems in countries like Iraq, where the oil for petrol comes from, by 2008 the price of petrol had risen to over £1 per litre. This was an increase of over 20%.

The cost of running his lorries has increased so much that Jonathan is now losing money. He is in danger of going bankrupt if he doesn't do something, for example raise his prices and/or reduce the number of lorries he has.

In groups

Imagine you are running a factory in the UK. Your profits have been hit by a global recession. This means the world economy is shrinking, and demand for your goods is falling. You need to do something, otherwise you will go out of business.

Study these four options and decide what you would do:

1 Negotiate with your suppliers to pay less for your raw materials. This will reduce your costs. But it also means that the workers who produce the raw materials in developing countries, who are already poorly paid, may have their wages cut.

2 Cut the amount of goods you are producing. This will means jobs will have to be cut and unemployment in the local area will rise.

3 Cut the price of your goods. This means that you will make less profit and you will have to cut the wages of your workforce too.

4 Try to sell the business to prevent yourself going bankrupt. But it may be hard to find a buyer, so you may have to reduce the price and sell the business for much less than you think it is worth.

For your file

"I'll do whatever I can to save my business, even if there are knock-on effects from any action I take to do so. It's not my fault there's a global recession and that unemployment will rise if I have to cut my workforce. After all, you've got to put yourself and your family first." Say what you think of this point of view.

19 You and the community

The school environment

> " It doesn't matter what the school looks like, it's only a school. "

> " The appearance of the school and grounds is important. They create the atmosphere of the school. "

> " It's up to everyone to look after the school and make sure the environment is pleasant. "

> " It's up to the local council to look after the school. "

> " People put up with things about the school environment that they'd never put up with in their own homes. "

> " Schools are like all public places. The environment suffers because people don't see it as their responsibility. "

 In groups

Discuss these comments about the school environment. How much do you think the school environment matters? Why do people put up with things at school that they wouldn't put up with at home? Whose responsibility is it to look after the school environment?

An environmental survey

Carry out a survey of the condition of the school's buildings and grounds. Draw up a chart like the one below and rate the condition of each area as either Good, Fair or Bad.

Area	Condition		
	Good	Fair	Bad
School gates/signs	❏	❏	❏
School drives/pathways	❏	❏	❏
School grounds/yards	❏	❏	❏
Playing fields	❏	❏	❏
Entrance hall	❏	❏	❏
Corridors	❏	❏	❏
Staircases	❏	❏	❏
Noticeboards	❏	❏	❏
Assembly hall	❏	❏	❏
Dining room	❏	❏	❏
Science labs	❏	❏	❏
Technology rooms	❏	❏	❏
Art room	❏	❏	❏
Music block	❏	❏	❏
Gymnasium	❏	❏	❏
Toilets	❏	❏	❏
General classrooms	❏	❏	❏

In groups

1 Show each other your surveys and discuss your views of the condition of the different areas of the school. Choose three areas which you would select as priority areas for improvement and share your ideas in a class discussion.

2 Imagine that it has been announced that schools can bid for up to £50,000 of lottery money for projects to improve the school environment. Discuss ideas for projects to improve your school environment. Choose one and draft a proposal to put to the rest of the class. Debate the various proposals, then vote to choose what your class's project would be.

3 Talk about what you could do to improve the appearance and atmosphere of your tutor group room. Organise a working party to investigate what any suggested improvements might cost and, if necessary, approach the appropriate school committee to apply for funds or hold a fundraising event. Then carry out the improvements.

The local environment

Wherever you live, your environment is important. Each day you make choices which have an effect on the environment. Taking action about the environment starts with doing things in your everyday life that help to cut down on waste, to conserve resources and to preserve the environment.

Local Agenda 21

Changing the way we live

What is Local Agenda 21?

Local Agenda 21 is a challenge for individuals, communities, businesses (in fact everyone) to get out, get active and get involved in changing the way we live at the moment.

Although the Earth is large, we are using up its resources faster than they can be replaced. We are polluting air, water and soil; we are creating more and more waste and destroying our environment in many ways.

In 1992 the UN conference on Environment and Development (the Earth Summit) was held in Rio, Brazil. One of the outcomes was Agenda 21, an action programme for sustainable development, signed by 179 nations including the UK.

It is not a fixed law, but an agreement between governments that they will promote sustainable development. Some of the topics included in Agenda 21 were promoting energy efficiency, preventing pollution, protecting endangered areas and reducing our consumption of the world's resources.

Local Agenda 21 is an initiative by local councils to get people involved in changing the way they live in order to promote sustainable development.

What is sustainable development?

Sustainable development means meeting our present needs without compromising the ability of future generations to meet their needs. It means making progress and improving the quality of our life without destroying the planet or having a bad effect on other people in the process.

To have a sustainable lifestyle we have to consider the resources we use, whether we are producing too much waste, how much pollution we produce, and how we affect the natural environment.

How can you become involved?

Local Agenda 21 challenges everyone to take responsibility for the problems the Earth is facing.

You can start by doing small things in your life towards sustainable living, such as turning the tap off when you clean your teeth, buying locally grown foods or recycling your cans and paper.

There may be a bigger project that you can become involved in, either by volunteering or taking part in a project organised by your school. There are many Local Agenda 21 projects that have been successful throughout the country (see pages 92–93).

In groups

On your own, make lists of things you can do individually to help save energy, cut down on waste and reduce pollution. Then compare your ideas in a group discussion.

Making a difference – changing places

Young people throughout the UK are making a difference to the environment by getting involved in projects organised by their schools, local councils and organisations such as the environmental charity Groundwork.

Groundwork supports communities in need, working with partners to help improve the quality of people's lives, their prospects and potential and the places where they live, work and play. Their vision is of a society of sustainable communities which are vibrant, healthy and safe, which respect the local and global environment and where individuals and enterprise prosper.

GROUNDWORK

CHANGING PLACES
CHANGING LIVES

Creating greener living spaces

'Before the project the garden was really horrible,' says Emma Bramwell, who worked on the Woodhey Road project in Plymouth. 'There was no way anyone could play safely there as it was full of syringes and broken glass. I've seen the boys who tried to play football in the garden get cut and bruised so many times. Because we had nowhere else to go we used to hang around on the street, but that got too dangerous as there was a lot of anti-social behaviour locally.

'I wanted somewhere safe for me and my friends to enjoy so I became a young volunteer with

Groundwork on the project to improve the garden and worked with some of the young children and helped to make sure they used the tools safely. The project brought lots of people together – some people who didn't even live on the estate came to see if they could join in because they'd heard rumours of how good it was going to be when it was finished.

'The project has made such a big difference, it attracts so many people and there's a lot less anti-social behaviour. I sometimes go to the garden and talk to the younger children – it's a good place to be.'

GIVING YOUNG PEOPLE A VOICE

Groundwork encourages young people to participate in making decisions about how to improve the local environment by getting them to identify needs and put forward proposals.

Mary Donkin (15) took part in 'Young Voices Durham', a project which enabled young people to express their views.

'Groundwork explained about Local Agenda 21. I hadn't heard of it before. I was interested in the environment but this made me more interested. People usually don't want to listen to what young people have to say about anything, they just go ahead and do things, and that's not what we want.

I think with Young Voices, if we can show that we care first, through doing little things to start with – for one thing we need a lot more litter bins in our village – if we can do that, then we can work our way up and change the major things. We're learning more about making ourselves heard.'

In groups

Investigate your local environment to identify what you think might be done to improve it. Use your IT skills to design a questionnaire which surveys people's opinions, to analyse the results and to draft a proposal. Either send a copy of your proposal to the local newspaper or invite a local councillor to come to the school to discuss your ideas.

Working with other young people

When Reuben Williams took part in a Groundwork Greater Nottingham youth project he realised just how little there was for young people to do. Inspired to make a difference, he volunteered as a youth worker to help improve things for other young people.

'I love working with young people and being able to pass on my skills and knowledge to them. I find being young myself helps a lot in building relationships as we share a lot of the same experiences.

'I work with young people of all ages. I've worked on projects with eight year olds and applied for funding to support a youth group. I've also helped design a play area and given the children the opportunity to say what they wanted to see and then helped to make it happen for them.

'Young people are always stereotyped as hoodies and trouble-makers and I don't think it's fair that we all get dragged into the same bracket. Young people do have a lot to offer to society and I'm proud to do things to support them and make more people aware of what we can do when given a chance.'

Go MADD
Organise a
Make A Difference Day

Make a Difference Day (MADD) is an annual event, usually a Saturday in October, organised by Community Service Volunteers, 237 Pentonville Road, London N1 9NJ. Thousands of people throughout the UK donate a few hours of their time to help the local community in some way, for example by cleaning graffiti off a bus shelter, cleaning up the local pond or doing some shopping for an older person.

In groups

Organise your own MADD event to take place for two to three hours one evening after school or on a Saturday morning.

First, make a list of the different things you could do to help the local community in the time available. Share your ideas in a class discussion. Draw up a class list of jobs and get people to volunteer for them. Appoint a committee of four or five people to act as a steering group to plan the event and to make sure that everyone involved knows what is expected of them.

After the event discuss how it went, talk about what went well and what you would do differently when organising a similar event in the future.

For your file

Write a press release to send to your local paper explaining how you organised your Make a Difference Day and what people did.

Attitudes towards older people

Ageism

To be old in Britain today is considered by many to be 'past it', 'over the hill' or a 'has been'.

Such attitudes towards older people are widespread in a society such as ours which values youth, beauty and material possessions.

For many people, who are not old themselves, growing old is something to be feared. It is seen as a time of loss and withdrawal from life, rather than as a natural development which occurs gradually over time. Yet if you were to ask older people how they feel about being 'old', they are likely to respond by saying that although they may look old, they still feel young inside.

Many of the negative images we have about older people are perpetuated by the media, which tends to portray them as victims of crime, poverty or neglect, or as figures of fun. To judge a person negatively simply because they are old is ageist.

Once you become aware of it, however, ageism is apparent in all areas of life – from the derogatory way we refer to older people as 'geriatrics', 'old fogies', or 'wrinklies' to the patronising way we treat older people as if they are children and need protecting. It also shows itself in the embarrassment and condemnation we express if an older person continues to have an interest in sex or if they prefer to dress in a style which we think is inappropriate for their age.

Ageism is at the root of some common assumptions we make about older people – that they are all stubborn and inflexible, dependent and institutionalised, senile and sexless.

Old age and memory loss

Many people who live to be very old become forgetful. For example, they may call people by their wrong name. This is considered to be a normal part of the ageing process.

Most older people retain their full mental powers until the end of their lives. However, some older people – between 10 and 20 per cent – suffer from varying degrees of dementia.

A person who suffers from dementia gets muddled and confused because they cannot remember things. They may forget where they put things, lose track of the time or the day of the week, and confuse objects, for example, mistaking the washing machine for the fridge. A person with severe dementia may be unable to recognise people or places.

There is no single cause of dementia. Scientists are carrying out research to try to understand dementia, but until it is fully understood in many cases it cannot be treated.

⠿ In groups

Study the article on ageism (left). Discuss how people regard older people and the way that they are presented by the media. Do you think society is ageist? Appoint a spokesperson and share your views in a class discussion.

Do you think that people undervalue the contribution that older people can make to society? Talk about older people that you know and about how they spend their time.

For your file

Write an article about the causes and effects of ageism. You could interview a number of older people and include their views in your article.

The problems faced by older people

Survey finds 'two worlds of old age'

A survey of older people's lifestyles found that one in four people aged 80 and over worries about being able to afford food, while two-thirds are concerned about paying for clothing or heating bills.

The findings are from a survey of 1,317 readers, aged 55 to over 90, of Yours, a magazine for older people.

While the majority, 90%, enjoyed retirement, a small but significant group faced a bleak old age.

The research provided evidence of 'two worlds of old age,' said the report's author, Alisoun Milne.

'If you live in your own home, in a shared household, with an occupational pension and are in the early stages of retirement, up to 75, you tend to be OK. But if you don't have that financial backing, live on your own, and are 80 or older, that tends not to be the case.'

Over half of those surveyed said they were unable to afford holidays, nearly 40% could barely buy presents, and a quarter found paying for household maintenance, heating and clothing problematic.

'Most older people enjoy retirement and contribute a great deal to their families and communities,' said Tessa Harding of Help the Aged. 'But the dire poverty of some is a real tragedy in a wealthy society.'

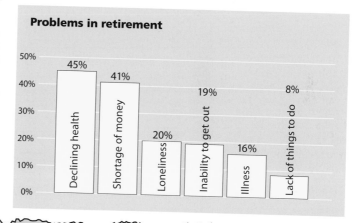

Problems in retirement

- Declining health — 45%
- Shortage of money — 41%
- Loneliness — 20%
- Inability to get out — 19%
- Illness — 16%
- Lack of things to do — 8%

In groups

Study the article and graph and discuss what you learn from them about the problems some older people face in old age.

Caring for older people

Many frail older people are only able to continue living in the community because they receive support from their carers and from services provided by the community, such as visiting care assistants, day care and respite care.

Older people who are frail or very disabled often cannot go out unless transport is provided for them, so transport is provided for them in special vehicles.

Once they become too frail or ill to be able to cope in their own homes, many older people have to be cared for in residential or nursing homes.

Social services departments spend an average of 64% of their budget for older people on supporting residents in residential and nursing homes. However, there are limited financial resources and older people can spend a lot of time in hospital before admission to residential or nursing care.

What role should the family play?

In groups

'Out of 1000 adults, 57% agreed that there was some obligation to care for older people in the family, 37% did not agree.' What role do you think the family should play in looking after older people?

What can the problems be when older people **a)** live with the family; **b)** live in their own homes? What other alternatives are there?

What can be done to support older people who live on their own and have no relatives?

An ageing population – society in the 21st century

🔲 In groups

Study the statistics in the article (below) and discuss how the age profile of society is changing.

Forecasts for the future

As the 21st century progresses there will be fewer younger people and more older people:

Between 1995 and 2040 the number of children under the age of ten will drop by nearly 20% – in the same period the number of people aged 65 will increase by over 60%.

The population of working age in the UK will drop sharply from 2011 onwards, just as the population of pensionable age rises fastest.

In 1961 there were almost four people of working age to support each pensioner; by 2040 there will be only two.

In 1951 there were 33 centenarians; in 2031 there will be 36,000.

By 2040 there will be 85% more people aged 80 and over than in 1995.

By 2040 there will be an extra 20 dependent pensioners for every 100 people of working age.

Admissions of older people to hospital are increasing by 4% a year, and over the next 35 years the proportion of people over 65 will rise by 30%.

It is projected that the number of disabled adults aged 60 and over will increase by almost 50% by 2031.

The population of pensionable age will rise to 12 million by 2021, and will peak at nearly 15.5 million around 2038.

How will life be different in the 21st century?

Young people born in the 1990s will be over 50 by the middle of the century. If you will be 50 or more in the year 2040 then the changes in society will affect you.

When the National Health Service was designed, life expectancy was around 50 years. Today it is 80 years.

By 2016 there will be almost 24 million households in Britain (23% more than in 1991) and more than one in three will consist of people living on their own.

By 2010 52% of workers will be doing some work at home. 8% of workers will be working 30 hours per week at home.

How do you think life will change because of these things?

In the 21st century, Britain will need 5 million extra homes. Do you think we should expand into the countryside to build the extra homes needed for the

There are unlikely to be major problems in the short to medium-term future of health and care, but significant challenges could face society after 2020. Medical advances in the 21st century will mean more and more conditions can be treated. But treatment costs money. The need to ration or control health service expenditure is increasingly being debated, and there are serious risks that the needs of older people will be seen as an unacceptable cost.

future?

Your retirement could last longer than your schooldays. Which do you agree with – individuals should be able to choose at what age they stop working, or retirement should be compulsory in order to allow younger people to have jobs?

By 2040 there will be only two working people to support every pensioner (as opposed to four working people in 1961). Will there be pensions for people (which means YOU) in the future? Without pensions, how would old people manage?

🔲 In groups

1 What does rationing mean? How can people be given a fixed allowance of medical treatment? Would that be a fair system?

2 Should people expect medical treatment if **a)** they don't have a healthy lifestyle, **b)** they take part in dangerous sports, or **c)** they travel to countries where there are health risks?

3 Do you think people would be prepared to pay more taxes to get whatever treatment they want, when they want?

4 Can you think of a system that is fair to everyone, whatever their age?

Thinking ahead

Study the stories on this page and discuss the questions and implications.

Liz's story

17 years old in the year 2010, a computer programmer. 'I'm training to be a computer programmer. I'll learn new skills as I go along, that way I've got a better chance of being employed.'

Q How can Liz help herself to stay employed?

47 years old in the year 2040, a project manager. 'I've started volunteering a few hours a week when I have a spell without work. They said I'd enjoy it and I can't believe how much I get out of it.'

Q Do we value Liz's volunteer work?

87 years old in the year 2080, still fit. 'I'm perfectly fit enough to work and I can't imagine giving it up. I do voluntary work. I'm helping myself and others at the same time.'

Q Why should Liz retire if she doesn't want to?

Patrick's story

17 years old in the year 2010, a shop assistant. 'I've just had my eyes corrected with laser surgery. No more glasses for me. It's done my confidence the world of good.'

Q Should Patrick get what healthcare he wants throughout his life?

47 years old in the year 2040, a manager. 'I had a small stroke this year and I've lost the use of my right arm. Magazines are always going on about eating healthy foods and taking exercise, but I never took any notice. Now I wish I had.'

Q Is it Patrick's responsibility to stay well with a healthy lifestyle?

87 years old in the year 2080. 'My daughter's got a life of her own and I don't want to depend on her. I'm lucky I've got someone to come in and help a few hours each day. My community pays her wages. I don't know what I'd do without them, the government can't pay for everyone.'

Q Who will Patrick want to look after him when he can't take care of himself?

For your file

Write about the changes that you think you will see during your lifetime as a result of the changing age profile of society. What, if anything, do you think you need to do to prepare for them?

The foods you eat

Most people have little idea of where their food comes from. In this article John Crace tells you some of the things that supermarkets would prefer to keep to themselves.

Spoilt for choice

Walk down any supermarket aisle and you would be hard pushed to realise that 800 million people in the world do not have enough food to meet their basic nutritional needs. The shelves groan with goodies, from the bare essentials such as sugar and bread, to the outright exotic, such as star fruit and ostrich steaks, and as soon as a gap appears a stacker appears from the storeroom to restock. The choice seems bewildering and the quantities limitless.

Maintaining this illusion carries a high price for producers, consumers and the environment. Producers often barely scrape a living as supermarkets squeeze them for rock-bottom prices for their goods. Consumers are often offered foods that have been sprayed by pesticides or treated with antibiotics or other additives so that producers can maximise the return from their fields and livestock. And the environment suffers because foods are air-freighted vast distances and then wrapped in non-biodegradable packaging.

Food miles

Many British consumers have become used to eating what they want when they want. Thanks to air transport, strawberries and runner beans are now available throughout the year at leading supermarkets. But the extra costs of out-of-season foods is not just reflected in the purchase price; the environment also suffers from added airline and road freight exhaust emissions.

Pesticides

Nearly all fruit and vegetables have been grown using pesticides. There are more than 300 chemicals approved for use in the UK, and farmers spray roughly 1 billion gallons of them each year on UK crops. An apple might have received 35 pesticide treatments by the time it reaches a supermarket.

Organic food

In 2006, organic food and drink sales in the UK reached £2 billion for the first time. The term 'organic' is a legal category, enforced by the government. Any food labelled organic must be grown or reared without the use of pesticides, artificial fertilisers, genetic modification and antibiotics. Weeds and pests are controlled by natural techniques and animals are reared in humane conditions.

Organic food is usually more expensive than mass-produced food, a reflection of the extra costs of its production. Despite the cost, an increasing number of people are converting to organic food because they believe it is better for animals and the environment and is both healthier and tastes better.

GM foods

Genetic engineering allows scientists to create new plants in the laboratory. It is done by altering the genes, the vital blueprints inside all living cells that give plants and animals their different characteristics. Most GM crops, however, are engineered to be resistant to pesticides, so that when they are sprayed on a field, everything but the crop will die.

The health effects of eating GM foods are as yet unknown, with the scientific community divided over possible risks to human health. There are also concerns that GM crops will cause genetic pollution by releasing pollen into the environment and transferring their genetic qualities to wild plants.

Antibiotics

Animals reared in intensive factory farms are more likely to become ill so they are routinely dosed with antibiotics. Almost all poultry, 80% of pigs and nearly half of all sheep and cattle raised in the UK are regularly treated in this way. The Soil Association campaigns against the overuse of antibiotics in factory farming, because it leads to antibiotic resistance in food poisoning bacteria, like salmonella. Scientific studies show that intensive farming has been implicated in the rise of the superbugs MRSA and Ecoli.

There is increasing evidence that the overuse of antibiotics is having harmful effects on humans. A report to the House of Lords Select Committee on Science and Technology concluded that 'there is a continuing threat to human health from imprudent use of antibiotics in animals' because antibiotic residues in meat are thought to lead to resistance to antibiotics in humans, rendering the drugs ineffective in fighting human illnesses.

In groups

1 Discuss what you learn from the information in this article about:
a) where our food comes from, b) how it is produced, and c) the effects that producing, packaging and transporting foods to stock our supermarket shelves have on the environment.

2 Discuss what is meant by 'organic foods'. Why are they considered by many people to be healthier than other foods? Do you think it is worth paying the extra price for organic foods?

3 What are the arguments for and against genetically modified foods? Do you think we should continue to develop them, or is the possibility that they will damage the environment too great a risk to take?

4 Discuss what you learn from the article about the problems that have resulted from giving antibiotics to animals.

5 What are your views on factory farming? Do you try to avoid eating foods that have been produced by factory farming? Is factory farming 'cruel and unnecessary'?

For your file

Write a letter to a newspaper expressing your views on one or more of the issues about the foods we eat that are raised in this article.

World hunger

Many people in the world do not get enough nourishment from the food they eat. **Malnutrition** is the term used to describe lack of nutrition in a person's diet. It is estimated that almost 750 million people suffer from malnutrition – more than twice the whole population of Europe.

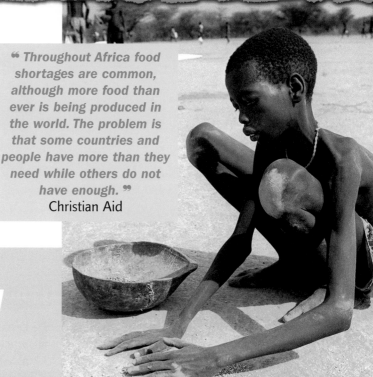

" *Throughout Africa food shortages are common, although more food than ever is being produced in the world. The problem is that some countries and people have more than they need while others do not have enough.* "
Christian Aid

Why do famines happen?

Famine is a crisis in which starvation from too little food results in a sharp increase in deaths in one place.

Hunger and malnutrition are more common than famine. One in five people don't get enough or the right kind of food to lead fully productive lives – they are vulnerable to disease, infection and parasites and grow up with weak bones and muscles. Malnutrition contributes to short life expectancy and for children is especially dangerous, affecting their strength and their ability to grow, to learn and to perform complex tasks.

Poverty

Poverty is the root cause of famine. People who live in poverty are always more vulnerable to natural disasters. When floods and droughts occur in wealthy countries, people don't starve because they don't rely on their land for food – they often have a salary, savings, insurance and, as a last resort the government has enough money and food to get emergency supplies through. But when you have little and lose even that – be it your crop or your house – there is nothing left to fall back on.

International trade

Food security is also affected by both local conditions and government policies. Many people argue that international trade policies are unfair and penalise poorer countries, many of which are caught in a debt trap which hits the poorest hardest. In Zambia almost half the population is undernourished. Yet still it bears one of the heaviest debt burdens in the world. For every man, woman and child, the Zambian government owes £437 to creditors.

War

War diverts valuable resources away from development. In a war-zone families cannot plant or tend crops, they have difficulty storing food for times of hardship, markets often close and the warring parties can prevent help reaching people. They are forced to leave their homes and to become refugees, relying for their survival on food aid.

▶

In groups

Study the information on these pages. Discuss the reasons people give for why there is hunger in Sub-Saharan Africa. Which are true? What are the real reasons why there is hunger in those countries?

For your file

Write a statement saying what you have learned from these pages about the reasons for hunger and malnutrition in some parts of the world and about how the problem could be solved.

Unequal shares

According to the United Nations the average person should eat no less than 2,400 calories a day. If a person's calorie intake is constantly below that level, they are likely to suffer from malnutrition.

Most of the people who suffer from malnutrition live in the poor countries in the developing world. The world produces enough grain to provide every person with 3,000 calories a day. And that doesn't include all the beans, fruit and vegetables that are grown. The problem is that the world's food is not distributed equally.

While millions of people do not get enough to eat, people in Western Europe, North America and Japan on average eat over 25% more calories than they need. In poorer countries, the richest 10% of the population eat more than twice the number of calories eaten by the poorest 20%.

Why are they hungry?

Half the people of Sub-Saharan Africa don't have enough to eat. Here are some reasons people give.

- People in Africa are lazy.
- African countries have difficult conditions for growing food.
- There is not enough food in the world.
- People have too many children.
- Some people in the world get more than their fair share of food.
- Nothing grows in Africa, it's too hot and never rains.
- Farmers in Africa need more pesticides and fertilisers.
- African farmers are not given a fair deal in the world market.
- Drought and famine are natural disasters which cannot be prevented.
- Farmers don't have enough good land on which to grow food.

Ten ways to beat world hunger

1 Increase the amount of aid to small farmers to help them stay on their land, for example, by giving them seeds and tools as well as food.

2 Cut down the amount of food which rich countries import from developing countries.

3 Reduce the amount of land used for growing cash crops.

4 Train farmers in methods that will increase the yield from their land.

5 Educate people so that they know which foods to grow and eat for a healthy diet.

6 Send more food aid to poor countries.

7 Introduce land reforms so that the land in developing countries is distributed more fairly.

8 Get more people in rich countries to change their eating habits, for example, by becoming vegetarians.

9 Cancel the debts which the governments of Third World countries owe to western banks.

10 Repair environmental damage and improve the quality of the land, for example, by tree-planting projects.

In groups

Discuss the ten suggestions for helping to solve the problem of world hunger. Put them in order of importance starting with the one you think will have the most long-term effect. Can you suggest other ways to help?

Water – a vital resource

The Water Crisis

A person needs about 5 litres of water a day for cooking and drinking.

But to stay clean and healthy a further 25–45 litres are needed per person.

Water is vital for all living things to survive – a few days without it and people die. In a rich country like the United Kingdom everyone has access to water. Yet for 80 countries – with 40 per cent of the world's population – lack of water is a constant threat.

Lack of water in many places in the world is an ever-worsening crisis. There is not enough water to drink and to keep crops and farm animals alive. Increases in population mean there is less water available for each person. Climate change, caused by pollution of the atmosphere, is making some countries which are already short of water even hotter and drier. Demand for water is doubling every 20 years.

The fresh clean water that is available is often wasted and misused. When people are poor they have no money to pump and pipe water. They cannot even afford proper houses. There are no sewage works to dispose of waste. As a result, what clean water there is gets mixed with dirty water and germs breed, causing illnesses. The United Nations estimates that

dirty water causes 80 per cent of disease in developing countries and kills 10 million people annually. The UN believes that the lack of clean water is becoming a terrible crisis for the world. Nations may go to war to fight to control the supply of water, as they have done in the past to fight for oil.

There are ways of solving the problem. The charity Water Aid starts at the beginning, with the poor people who need the water most. These people have no access to expensive technology so all schemes are kept simple. Wells are dug and maintained with hand tools. Hand pumps can be provided so that whole villages can be supplied with clean water. Water can be brought in by pipeline and gravity does the rest.

Just as importantly, simple sewage schemes are organised so that dirty water is kept away from the clean. Many hours of work in carrying water is avoided, children stay healthy, and a huge problem gets smaller.

How much do you know about water?

Do this test-yourself quiz, then check the answers (see page 106).

1 How much of our bodies is made up of water?
a. 10% **b.** 70% **c.** 25%

2 What percentage of the world's population does not have access to safe, clean water?
a. 10% **b.** 25% **c.** 70%

3 How much water does it take to flush the toilet?
a. 2·5 litres **b.** 9·5 litres **c.** 19 litres

4 How much water on average does someone in the UK and Ireland use every day for drinking, washing and cooking?
a. 135 litres **b.** 50 litres **c.** 15 litres

5 Which of these diseases are caused by a lack of safe, clean water and poor sanitation?
a. dysentery **b.** diarrhoea **c.** cholera

6 How many people will die every minute in the Third World from diseases caused by unsafe water?
a. 10 **b.** 1 **c.** 30

7 Traditionally women in Africa and Asia collect the water for the whole family, carrying it up to several miles on their heads or their backs. What is the average weight of the water they carry?
a. 4 kg **b.** 20 kg **c.** 80 kg

8 How much money will provide someone in the Third World with safe water for life?
a. £2.50 **b.** £10 **c.** £50

From *Water Works*, CAFOD

Billions without a toilet or safe water

Billions of people around the world lack even the most basic sanitation or clean water. That's why leading Christian relief and development agency Tearfund is calling on Prime Minister Gordon Brown to lead the international community in urgent action.

Tearfund's senior policy adviser on water Laura Webster said: 'The irony is that in 2008, the UN's year of sanitation, 2.6 billion people are still without sanitation facilities and 1.1 billion others lack safe water.'

Lack of water and sanitation is something that Justice from the Kabale District in south-west Uganda knows all too well – and it has affected his children the most.

Justice said: 'My children have had to spend hours each day fetching water from the lake. They missed school and got sick because they didn't have enough water for hand-washing.'

The carcasses of fishes killed by cyanide flowing down the Tisza river from a Romanian mine.

Water wars

Most of the world's great rivers flow across continents, often through several countries. Along their banks are many cities and thousands of farmers relying on irrigation to grow crops. Each year the demand for water grows. Governments decide to dam rivers for hydroelectricity schemes or to store water for the dry season. Downstream it means people who relied on that water for their own use are deprived of it.

One of the best examples is the Nile and its tributaries which flow through seven countries. Egypt uses all the water the Nile can produce to irrigate the desert lands. Sudan, which is upstream, has agreed not to take any more. But some of the poorer countries even further inland – Eritrea, Ethiopia and Uganda – all need more water for growing populations but dare not take it. Egypt has warned them: 'Take any more and we will send in the army.'

In groups

Discuss all the ways that we use water in our homes. How would your life be different if you did not have a water supply in your home, but had to walk 4–5 kilometres to fetch your water from a stand-pipe or a well, using 10 litre containers?

Study the information on these pages and discuss what you learn from them about the problems many people in the world have of getting sufficient clean water. Why is the demand for water likely to lead to international conflicts in the future?

Assessing your progress and achievements

The aim of this unit is to help you to think about what progress you have made and what you have achieved during Year 8. It gives you the chance to discuss your progress with your tutor, to write a statement about your achievements and to look ahead and set yourself targets for what you hope to achieve in Year 9.

Your subjects

Think about the effort you have made in each of your subjects and what your progress and achievements have been.

For your file

Make a list of all the subjects you are studying and use a five-point scale to give yourself grades for effort and progress in each subject:
1 Excellent   2 Good   3 Satisfactory
4 Poor   5 Unsatisfactory.
Then write a brief comment on your work and progress in your subjects. Give reasons for the grades you have given yourself, and evidence to support your views of your progress and achievements in each subject.

Your skills

Think about your progress in the skills that you are learning as a result of the work which you do in your different subjects. These are the skills:

�֎ Communication skills   �֎ Numeracy skills
✖ Study skills   ✖ Problem-solving skills
✖ Personal and social skills   ✖ ICT skills.

For your file

Think about your skills and write a short comment on each one, saying how much you think you have improved that skill during the past year – a lot, quite a lot, only a little. Support your statement by referring to something you have done during the year.

Your activities

Think about the activities you do and what you have achieved in both school and out-of-school activities.

In pairs

Each make a list of all the activities you have taken part in this year, both inside and outside school. Include details of events organised by clubs and societies that you belong to, sports activities, drama and musical activities and any school events that you have been involved in.

Show your list to your partner and discuss any events that were particular highlights because of what you achieved in them.

For your file

Write a short statement giving details of your most significant achievements in your activities during the year.

Your attitude and behaviour

Think about what your attitude and behaviour have been like during the year.
- Have your attendance and punctuality been good?
- Has your behaviour been good
  a) in lessons, b) around the school?
- Have you kept up-to-date with your work and handed it in on time?
- Have you volunteered for things and played as full a part as you could in the life of the school?

For your file

Write a short comment summing up your attitude and behaviour during Year 8.

Discussing your progress

Arrange a meeting with your tutor. Show them what you have written about your subjects and your skills and discuss your progress and achievements in Year 8. Compare your own views with those that your teachers have made on subject reports or subject review sheets. Together decide what your strengths and weaknesses are at present.

Talk about the activities in which you have taken part and what you consider to be your significant achievements, and discuss what you wrote about your attitude and behaviour.

During the meeting listen carefully to what your tutor has to say. Add anything to your statements which your tutor thinks you have missed out. Note down any comments they make in which they disagree with your assessment, either because they think you have been too harsh on yourself, or because they think that you have overestimated the amount of progress you have made.

Recording your achievements

Use a word processor to draft a statement as a record of your progress and achievements during Year 8. Include comments on your subjects, your key skills, your activities and your attitude and behaviour.

Before you put your record in your progress file, show it to your tutor. Agree any changes that your tutor thinks you should make, so that your final statement is what you both consider to be an accurate record of your progress and achievements.

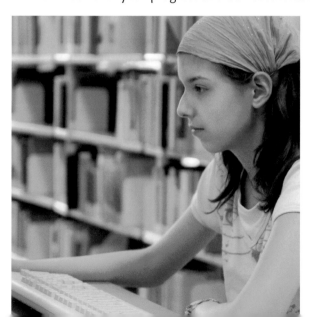

Setting targets

Use your meeting with your tutor to set targets for the future. Assessing what has gone well can help you to identify which subjects and skills you need to improve. When you have identified a subject or a skill that you need to improve, you can set yourself a target and draw up an action plan.

Making an action plan

Step 1 Decide which skills and subjects you would most like to try to improve in Year 9. Discuss with your tutor what you would need to do and the things you would need to change in order to improve in that subject or skill.

Step 2 Together with your tutor agree two or three targets which you both think would be realistic for you to set yourself during Year 9.

Step 3 Draw up an action plan for each of your targets. Think carefully about the various things you need to do in order to achieve a particular target and plan how you are going to achieve it step by step. Give yourself plenty of time to achieve it and set yourself deadlines by which you plan to achieve each step.

State clearly what your aim is, then list the steps you are going to take in order to achieve your goal. Here is the action plan that Gaby drew up in order to try to improve her work in History:

Aim: To get a higher grade in History in Year 9.

Steps

1. Use more sources when I'm asked to find out about a topic.

2. Go to the library and look for information in books, on CD-ROMs and the Internet.

3. Make better notes which are focused on the question instead of just copying whole paragraphs from the book.

4. Use more evidence to support the points I make in my written work.

5. Do my History homework in plenty of time instead of at the last minute.

6. Ask Miss Wilks if I can see her once a month to keep a check on how I'm doing.

In pairs

Show each other your action plans. Discuss any problems you think you may have in trying to achieve them and what you might do to overcome them.

Index

Answers to quiz on page 102: 1 b, **2** b, **3** b, **4** a, **5** all of them, **6** a, **7** b (the weight of 20 bags of sugar), **8** b (to provide wells and water engineers).

Acknowledgments

The following permissions to reproduce material are gratefully acknowledged:

'Coping with shyness' (p8) is adapted from 'pain of shyness' in T2, *The Daily Telegraph*, 23 October 1999 © Telegraph Group Limited, 1999, used with permission; 'Coping with classroom mistakes' (p9) is adapted from *Wise Guides, Self Esteem* by Anita Naik, published by Hodder & Stoughton, reprinted with permission of Hodder & Stoughton Publishers; 'Learning from your mistakes' (p9) is from *Growing Up*; 'Drugs – facts and fictions' (p10) is adapted from pp32-35 of *Wise Guides: Drugs* by Anita Naik, published by Hodder & Stoughton, reprinted with permission of Hodder & Stoughton Publishers; 'Is cannabis safe?' (p10) and 'Drugs and the law' (p12) are taken from *The Score – Facts about Drugs* © Health Education Authority, used with permission; 'How to turn down drugs and stay friends' (p13) is from pp36-38 of *Wise Guides: Drugs* by Anita Naik, published by Hodder & Stoughton, reprinted with permission of Hodder & Stoughton Publishers; extract (p14) is from *Roots of the Future*, published by Commission for Racial Equality, reprinted with permission; 'Stereotype' (p15) by John Agard is from *Mangoes and Bullets*, published by Pluto Press, 1985, reprinted by kind permission of John Agard c/o Caroline Sheldon Literary Agency; 'Negative stereotyping' (p16) and 'The Press' (p17) are from *Life Files: Racism* by Jagdish Gundara and Roger Hewitt, published by Evans Brothers Limited © 1999 Evans Brother Limited, used with permission; 'Does the media stereotype Africans?' (p17) is from 'Answer the question – stereotyped Africans' (p17) is from 'Answer the question – stereotyped Africans' with kind permission of Headliners, www.headliners.org; 'Fruit Machine Facts' (p19) is from 'Shout report – gambling' in *Shout* issue 127, published by D.C. Thomson & Co. Ltd © D.C. Thomson & Co. Ltd, reprinted with permission; 'Problem gambling' (p21) is adapted from *A Certain Bet*, published by GamCare, reproduced with permission; 'Responsible gambling' (p21) is from *Gambling! A Guide for Young People*, published by GamCare, reproduced with permission; news extracts (pp24-25) are from *Daily Mail*, 27 Sept 2008, reproduced with permission of Solo Syndication; 'Dealing with divorce' (p26) is from *Girls Know Best*, compiled by Michelle Roehm, published by Beyond Words Publishing Inc © 1997 Beyond Words Publishing Inc, Hillsboro, Oregon, USA, used with permission; 'We had to move to a small flat' and 'I get the best of both worlds' (p28) are from *Dealing with Family Break-up* by Kate Haycock, published by Wayland Publishers, reprinted with permission of Hodder & Stoughton Publishers; 'I want to be with my mates' (p28) and quotes from Janet, Jason and Rachel (p29) are from *Caught in the Middle* by Alys Swan-Jackson, published by Piccadilly Press, reprinted with permission of Piccadilly Press; 'How to cope with step-parents' (p29) is from 'Coping with step-families' from *Shout* issue 118, published by D.C. Thomson & Co. Ltd © D.C. Thomson & Co. Ltd, reprinted with permission; 'What is child abuse?' (p32) and 'What happens next?' (p33) are from *Speaking out about Abuse – What Every Young Person Should Know* produced by NSPCC London, reprinted with permission; 'I feel so guilty and ashamed' (p33) is from *Sussed and Streetwise* by Jane Goldman, published by Piccadilly Press, reprinted with permission of Piccadilly Press; 'Staying safe in the street' and 'Safety on buses' (p34) are from *Respect – Your Life Your Choice*, published by National Children's Safety Books, used with permission of The Access Partnership, Stockport; 'Safety in public places', 'If someone talks to you persistently' and 'The golden rule of self-defence' (p35) are from *Stand Up for Yourself* by Helen Benedict, published by Hodder & Stoughton, reprinted with permission of Hodder & Stoughton Publishers and Helen Benedict; 'Cycling Safely' (p36) is from *English Direct 1* by John Foster and Keith West © HarperCollins Publishers; 'Police duties and police powers' (p38) and 'Helping the police' (p39) are from *Young Citizen's Passport – Your Guide to the Law*, published by Hodder & Stoughton, reprinted with permission of Hodder & Stoughton Publishers; 'Reprimands, warnings and prosecutions' (p39) is from the leaflet 'Youth Justice', produced by the Metropolitan Police Youth Justice Task Force, 1999, reprinted with permission of the Metropolitan Police Service; 'Doing a good job?' (p41) is from *Teen Law*, published by Quest, A Young Enterprise company, Queen Elizabeth Boys School, used with permission; 'The secret of making friends' (p42) is from *Friends and Enemies* by Anita Naik, published by Hodder & Stoughton, reprinted with permission of Hodder & Stoughton Publishers; 'Growing Apart' (p43) is from *Shout Summer Special* 1999, published by D.C. Thomson & Co. Ltd © D.C. Thomson & Co. Ltd, reprinted with permission; 'The Rules of Friendship' (p43) is from *Play Stay Keep Safe*, published by National Children's Safety Books, used with permission of The Access Partnership, Stockport; 'How much are you influenced by your friends?' (p44) is adapted from *Exploring Healthy Sexuality* by Cathy Jewitt, Family Planning Association, used with permission; 'Gangs – know the facts' (p45) is from *Shout* issue 105, published by D.C. Thomson & Co. Ltd © D.C. Thomson & Co. Ltd, reprinted with permission; 'Is advertising good or bad?' (p46) and 'The commercial break' (p48) are from *Third Stages* by Jim Sweetman, published by Collins Educational, reprinted with permission of HarperCollins Publishers and Jim Sweetman; 'Advertising and children' (p47) is from Appendix 3 of the Radio Authority's Advertising and Sponsorship Code, March 1997, reprinted with the kind permission of the Radio Authority; 'Getting a piece of the action' (p52) is from Samantha Graham; extract (p53) from *Print-Base 1* by John Foster, published by Nelson Thornes Ltd; 'What's all the fuss about?' (p54) is adapted from *Drugs – Reference Point Series* by Anita Ganeri, published by Scholastic Limited, used with permission; 'Kerry's story' (p60) is from *Shout* issue 116, published by D.C. Thomson & Co. Ltd © D.C. Thomson & Co. Ltd, reprinted with permission; 'Valerie's story' (p61) is adapted from 'Stolen childhood' by Anita Chaudhuri, from *19*, 19 October 1991; 'Living with someone who drinks – how to cope' (p61) is from *Wise Guides: Drugs* by Anita Naik, published by Hodder & Stoughton, reprinted with permission of Hodder & Stoughton Publishers; 'The Henry Box School – school uniform' (p65) is from 'The School Uniform', the Henry Box School; 'Dentists warn of piercing perils' (p69) adapted from the article 'Dentists warn of illnesses linked to tongue piercing' in *The Daily Telegraph*, 21 July 1999, 'Sickening sight!' (p69) from the letters pages of T2, *The Daily Telegraph*, 12 June 1999, and 'Should body piercing be banned?' (p69) adapted from an article in T2, *The Daily Telegraph*, 5 June 1999, © Telegraph Group Limited, used with permission; Zoe Rockcliffe's quote (p69) is from 'A piercing cry of anger' in *The Guardian*, 25 February 1998 © The Guardian, used with permission; 'Sex and Contraception… Your questions answered' (p72) is adapted from '50 Sex Questions Answered' in *Mizz* © 1997 Mizz; 'I'm worried about protection' (p73) is from 'Your top 50 problems solved' by Tricia Keitman in *Mizz* © 1997 Mizz; 'The rhythm method' and 'Withdrawal' (p73) and 'Sex myths' (p75) are from *Wise Guides: Sex* by Anita Naik, published by Hodder & Stoughton, reprinted with permission of Hodder & Stoughton Publishers; 'Sexual rights and responsibilities' (p74) is adapted from *Stand Up for Yourself* by Helen Benedict, published by Hodder & Stoughton, reprinted with permission of Hodder & Stoughton Publishers and Helen Benedict; 'What is acceptable in a sexual relationship?' (p75) is adapted from *Exploring Healthy Sexuality* by Carey Jewitt, published by Family Planning Association, used with permission; 'How It Began' (p76) is from 'Gaining strength through unity' by Larry Elliott, from *Guardian Education*, 26 February 1995 © the Guardian, used with permission; 'The Single Market' (p77) and 'What the EU does to protect the environment' (p79) are from *What exactly is Europe?* By Muriel Lamb, published by The European Commission © 1997 the European Commission, used with permission; 'European Institutions' (p80) is from *Democracy in Action* by Simon Foster, published by HarperCollins Publishers, reprinted with permission by Simon Foster and HarperCollins Publishers; 'Should Britain join the Euro?' (p83) by Philip Johnston, is from T2 in *The Daily Telegraph*, 26 June 1999 © Telegraph Group Limited, used with permission; the environmental survey chart (p90) is from *Personal and Social Education and Cross Curricular Themes Year 10.* text © Burnage High School and Manchester City Educational Committee 1994, published by Evans Brothers Ltd, 2A Portman Mansions, Chiltern Street, London W1M 1LE, used with permission; 'Changing the way we live' (p91) is from *Local Agenda 21 Handbook 1999* published by Oxford City Council, reprinted with permission; extracts (pp92-93) are adapted from text provided by Groundwork, used with permission; 'Ageism' (p94) is adapted from information supplied by Help the Aged; 'Survey finds two worlds or old age' and the graph 'Problems in retirement' (p95) are adapted from 'Half over 80s exist on £80 a week or less' by Sarah Hall in *The Guardian*, 5 Oct 1999 © The Guardian, used with permission; 'An ageing population' (pp96-97) is from *Future Forecasts – Statistics Book* and *Thinking Ahead – Assembly Book* in the Debate of Age Series coordinated by Age Concern, used with permission; 'The foods you eat' (pp98-99) is from 'Spoilt for choice' by John Crace, In *Guardian Education*, 1 February 2000 © the Guardian, used with permission; 'Why do famines happen?' (p100) is adapted from an article 'Why do famines happen?' in *Global Express Edition 11* © 2007 Development Education Project; 'Unequal shares' (p101) is from *Fighting Famine, Beating Hunger* produced by Christian Aid, reprinted with permission; 'The Water Crisis' (p102) and 'Water Wars' (p103) are from 'Water, water everywhere but not a drop to drink' by Paul Brown in *Guardian Education*, 18 March 1997 © The Guardian, reprinted with permission; 'How much do you know about water?' (p102) is from *Youth Topics* issue 27 – *Water Works*, published by CAFOD London, reprinted with permission; 'Billions without a toilet or safe water' is from 'World Water Day? Not for the billions without a toilet or safe water' © 2009 Tearfund UK, www.tearfund.org;

Whilst every effort has been made to contact the copyright holders, this has not proved possible in every case.

Photographs

The publishers would like to thank the following for permission to reproduce photographs (page numbers are in brackets and are followed, where necessary, by t-top, b-bottom, l-left, r-right, c-centre):

Hunter Freeman/GettyOne Stone (6); Howard Grey/GettyOne Stone (8); Zigy Kaluzny/GettyOne Stone (9); Nikki Gibbs/Bubble Photo Library (10); Press Association/European Press Agency (11); David Montford/Photo Fusion (12); Laurence Monneret/GettyOne Stone (13, 44); Eric gaillard/Reuters/Corbis (14t); Felipe Trueba/epa/Corbis (14c); Jan Woitas/dpa/Corbis (14b); Chris Brown/Action-Plus (p15); Rune Hellestad/Corbis (16); Ad Mansard/istockphoto.com (17l); Sean Warren/istockphoto.com(17r); istockphoto.com (18, 21t, 24t. 40b, 67, 79, 84-85, 88, 89, 101, 105, 57b, 59, 94l); Tim Ockenden/Press Association (19); Stefan Klein/istockphoto.com (20l); Mark Campbell/Photofusion (20r); Steve Taylor/GettyOne Stone (21b); Lori Adamski/GettyOne Stone (22); Ben Radford/Corbis (23t); Bernstein/Frank Spooner Pictures (23b); Vladimir Melnik/istockphoto.com (24b); Fred Palmieri/istockphoto.com (26); Bruce Ayres/GettyOne Stone (27); Ute Klaphake/Photofusion (28); Stewart Cohen/GettyOne Stone (29); Renee Lee/istockphoto.com (30); Clarissa Leahy/GettyOne Stone (33); Angela Hampton/Bubbles Photo Library (34t); Paul Baldesare/Photofusion (34b); Ian West/Bubbles Photo Library (35); Elena Elisseeva/istockphoto.com (36); Matt Cardy/Stringer/Getty Images (38); David Tothill/Photofusion (39); Andy Rain/epa/Corbis (40t); G. Montgomery/Photofusion (41); David Stewart/GettyOne Stone (42); Marc Dophin/GettyOne Stone (43); Lihee Avidan/Getty Images (45); Matthew Fearn/Press Association (46); Kenneth C. Zirkel/istockphoto.com (47); Deborah Davis/GettyOne Stone (48); Neil Munns/Press Association (49); John Walmsley (50l, 70); Andy Sacks/GettyOne Stone(50r); Tim Pannell/Corbis (52); Ian Tyler/istockphoto.com (54); Juan Silva/istockphoto.com (55t); Nathan Maxfield/istockphoto.com (55b); Brad Wieland/istockphoto.com (57t); Ian O'Leary/GettyOne Stone (60); Penny Tweedie/GettyOne Stone (61); Jennie Woodcock/Bubbles Photo Library (62); Ian Shaw/GettyOne Stone (61l); Jacob Wackerhausen/istockphoto.com (62r); Gina Glover/Photofusion (64); Kevin Russ/istockphoto.com (66);Chris Schmidt/istockphoto.com (68, 97t); Sandra Kim/istockphoto.com (69); Juan Monino/istockphoto.com (71t); Gordon Dixon/istockphoto.com (71b); Peter Cade/GettyOne Stone (72); Peter Correz/GettyOne Stone (73); Simon Norfolk/GettyOne stone (74); Oleksandr Kramarenko/istockphoto.com (75); Sean Warren/istockphoto.com (77); Andy Drysdale/Press Association (78); Chris Hepburn/istockphoto.com (81); Press Association/European Press Agency (82, 83); Masterfile (84); Graeme Robertson/Getty Images (85t); Siewart Falko/dpa/Corbis (85b); image courtesy of Green Works (87); Kurt Gordon/istockphoto.com (90); Jan Rysavy/istockphoto.com (91l); Bryan Lever/istockphoto.com (91r); photos courtesy of Groundwork (92-93); Stephen Rose/GettyOne Stone (94r); Alexander Raths/istockphoto.com (96); Jennifer Trenchard/istockphoto.com (97b); Frank van den Bergh/istockphoto.com (98l); LV Design/istockphoto.com (98r); Darko Dozet/istockphoto.com (99l); Dan Harmeson/istockphoto.com (99r); Press Association/European Press Agency (100, 102, 103t); Nigel Dickenson/Still Pictures (103b); Jane Norton/istockphoto.com (104).

Illustrations

(31) Corinne Pearlman